W9-DHG-887

SAMUEL BECKETT

WORLD DRAMATISTS
In the same series:

WORLD DRAMATISTS

SAMUEL BECKETT

RONALD HAYMAN

WITH HALFTONE ILLUSTRATIONS

FREDERICK UNGAR PUBLISHING CO.
NEW YORK

First American publication 1973

© *1968, 1973 by Ronald Hayman*
Printed in the United States of America
Library of Congress Catalog Card Number: 72-79935
Designed by Edith Fowler
ISBN 0-8044-2373-3 (cloth)

ACKNOWLEDGMENTS

The Author would like to thank Catherine Barton, Martha Crewe, John Peter, Charles Tomlinson, and Irving Wardle for their help in reading typescripts and making useful comments, when the series was in preparation.

The Author and Publishers wish to thank the following for permission to include quotations from the publications listed below:

All That Fall, Waiting for Godot, Endgame, Krapp's Last Tape, Embers, Happy Days, Play: Samuel Beckett and Faber & Faber Ltd; "Burnt Norton" from *Collected Poems of T. S. Eliot, 1909–62:* Faber & Faber Ltd.

CONTENTS

CHRONOLOGY

1906   Born near Dublin on Good Friday, second
            son of a Protestant quantity surveyor.

1923–37   At Trinity College, Dublin. First class honors
            in B.A. degree in Modern Literature (French
            and Italian). Games: cricket, golf, and chess.

1926   First visit to France—a bicycle tour of the
            Loire.

1928   Began teaching at Campbell College, Belfast.

1928–30   Lecteur at École Normale Supérieure in
            Paris. Met James Joyce.

1930   *Whoroscope* published in Paris.

1930–32   Assistant lecturer in French, Trinity College,
            Dublin.

1933   His father died, leaving him an annuity.

1937   Settled in Paris.

1942   Narrow escape from Gestapo after working
            with a resistance group.

1942–44   Worked as an agricultural laborer and
            wrote *Watt*.

1944–46   After revisiting Ireland to see his family,
            worked as interpreter and storekeeper at an
            Irish Red Cross hospital in Normandy.

1946–50   Started writing in French, producing in rapid
            succession the three novels of his trilogy

Molloy, *Malone Dies*, and *The Unnamable*, as well as the plays *Eleuthéria* and *Waiting for Godot*.

1950   His mother died.

1959   *Embers* won Italia Prize.

1961   International Publishers' Prize shared with Borges.

1968   Directed *Endgame* in Schiller Theater Werkstatt, Berlin.

1969   Directed *Krapp's Last Tape* for Schiller Theater, with Martin Held.

1969   Awarded Nobel Prize for Literature.

1971   Directed *Happy Days* for Schiller Theater.

SAMUEL BECKETT

The vogue for Beckett started with the success of *Waiting for Godot*, which was produced in Paris in January 1953. It was his first play, apart from one called *Eleuthéria*, written in 1947 but never published or performed. He had already written a volume of short stories, *More Pricks Than Kicks*, published in 1934, and two novels: *Murphy*, which appeared in 1938, and *Watt*, which was not published until 1953, although he finished writing it in 1944.

After *Watt* he turned to writing in French, and in 1945 he started a novel called *Mercier et Camier*. This was never finished but some of the extracts which have been published* show how the dialogue of the male couple anticipates the exchanges between Vladimir and Estragon in *Waiting for Godot*.

This is worth looking into, said Camier.

We shall confer, said Mercier, we shall make a broad survey.

Before venturing any further, said Camier.

* In *Samuel Beckett* by Hugh Kenner and *The Novels of Samuel Beckett* by John Fletcher.

Exactly, said Mercier.

To do that we need to be in complete possession of all our many faculties, said Camier.

That would be preferable, said Mercier.

And are we? said Camier.

Are we what? said Mercier.

In complete possession of our faculties, said
Camier.

I trust not, said Mercier.

We are in need of sleep, said Camier.

Exactly, said Mercier.

This short passage is characteristic of the style that
Beckett went on to develop. It is striking how one
man's remark continues the other's line of thought, as
if their minds overlapped, and how both speakers
seem at the same time to enjoy the words and yet to
hold back from them, to use sugar tongs on each
phrase, as if afraid of infection by commitment to
meaning. So they take refuge in a pedantry which they
ridicule at the same time. A phrase like "in complete
possession of all our many faculties" is made to sound
all the more grotesque for being repeated. Twenty-two
years later, in *All That Fall*, another couple, Dan and
Maddy Rooney, both find their own way of talking
rather bizarre.

MRS. ROONEY: No no, I am agog, tell me all, then
we shall press on and never pause, never pause,
till we come safe to haven.

MR. ROONEY: Never pause . . . safe to haven . . .
Do you know, Maddy, sometimes one would
think you were struggling with a dead language.

MRS. ROONEY: Yes indeed, Dan, I know full well
what you mean, I often have that feeling, it is
unspeakably excruciating.

MR. ROONEY: I confess I have it sometimes myself, when I happen to overhear what I am
saying.

MRS. ROONEY: Well, you know, it will be dead, in
time, just like our own poor dear Gaelic, there
is that to be said.

Whether explicitly, as here, or implicitly, and
whether writing in French or in English, Beckett's
concern is always partly with the language itself, and
in criticizing his work, it is particularly important to
start and end with the language.

The object of this book is to assess his importance as
a playwright, but I think it would be a mistake to
leave his other books out of account. I shall not attempt a complete survey of them, as I shall of the
plays, but it will often be helpful to refer to his novels
and to his book on Proust. The poetry is disappointing
and fairly negligible. But the more familiar you become with Beckett's other work—the novels, the plays,
the short stories, the criticism, and the scripts for the
film and the television play—the more you come to see
the whole body of it as a self-consistent world which
has only limited connections with the world outside
but intricate cross-references and inbred relationships
within itself. The narrator-heroes of the novels are
partly reincarnations of each other and often refer to
each other by name. The novels and plays share many
of the same preoccupations, often expressing them
through the same motifs, and his book on Proust
(1931) throws a lot of light on his own later work.

Most of his important work was written about
the same time as *Waiting for Godot*. *Murphy* and
Malone Dies were written just before it, and *The
Unnamable* just after it (1947–9). This prolific period

ended with the *Textes pour rien* (1950). Beckett then felt that he had been saying the same thing again and again. "There's no way to go on," he declared in 1956. "At the end of my work there's nothing but dust."

But it was in that year, 1956, that he ended his five years of silence with *Endgame* (in French) and his first radio play *All That Fall* (in English). *Krapp's Last Tape* was also written in English, in 1958, and *Embers*, a second radio play in 1959. Since then he has written very little—*How It Is* in 1960 and *Happy Days*, the first full-length play to be written in English, in 1961. There were two more radio plays, *Words and Music*, 1962, and *Cascando*, 1963, the year which also saw the premiere of his one-act play *Play* in Ulm. Since his television play *Eh, Joe* (1965), all his work has been on a very small scale. Fictions like *Imagination Dead Imagine* and *Le Dépeupleur* run to only a few pages; the dramatic work *Come and Go* runs for two and a half minutes, and *Breath* lasts about thirty seconds. *Not I* lasts a few minutes. But Beckett has so often seemed to have reached the end of the line, only to return on a new tack, that this could well happen again.

PLAYS

Waiting for Godot

The achievement of *Waiting for Godot* is that like no other play it crystallizes inaction into a dramatic action. The effect it has on an audience is rather like the effect that the piano tuners have on Watt in the novel by that name.

What distressed Watt in this incident of the Galls father and son, and in subsequent similar incidents, was not so much that he did not know what had happened, for he did not care what had happened, as that nothing had happened, that a thing that was nothing had happened, with the utmost formal distinctness, and that it continued to happen, in his mind, he supposed, though he did not know exactly what that meant, and though it seemed to be outside him, before him, about him, and so on, inexorably to unroll its phases, beginning with the first . . . and ending with the last . . . and omitting none, uninvoked, at the most unexpected moments, and the most inopportune. Yes, Watt could not accept . . . that nothing had happened, with all the clarity and solidity of something, and that it revisited him in such a way that he was forced to submit to it all over again, to

7

hear the same sounds, see the same lights, touch the same surfaces, and so on, as when they had first involved him in their unintelligible intricacies. If he had been able to accept it, then perhaps it would not have revisited him, and this would have been a great saving of vexation, to put it mildly. But he could not accept it, could not bear it. One wonders sometimes where Watt thought he was. In a culture-park?

The action of most plays can be summed up in a few sentences, but not the action of *Godot*. One critic summarized the plot by saying: "Nothing happens, twice." But how can we describe the nothing that happens? The act of waiting is itself a contradictory combination of doing nothing and doing something. Vladimir and Estragon do not actually do anything, and they are agreed right from the beginning that there is nothing they can do. "Nothing to be done" is the play's opening line, and although Estragon is talking about his boot, which he's trying to take off, Vladimir's answer immediately makes the line we've just heard into a general pronouncement about their situation in life:

I'm beginning to come round to that opinion. All my life I've tried to put it from me, saying, Vladimir, be reasonable, you haven't yet tried everything. And I resumed the struggle.

But now that he has tried everything, or thinks he has, at least everything he's capable of trying, there's nothing left to do except wait for Godot. Which is the same as doing nothing, except that if you are waiting, you are not free to go. Estragon keeps forgetting that and wanting to go, and each time Vladimir has to stop him. They have the same exchange of lines each time, like a refrain:

> Let's go.
> We can't.
> Why not?
> We're waiting for Godot.
> Ah!

They wait for Godot both days that we see them, and they are going to come back to wait for him again the next day, and no doubt the day after that. We can be fairly sure they were waiting for him on the previous day and the day before that and the day before that. Godot will never come but they will never be sure that he is not coming because there will always seem to be some reason for hoping that he will come tomorrow. And there will always be the possibility that he came today and that they failed to recognize him. Perhaps Pozzo was Godot. It has even been suggested (by Norman Mailer in *Advertisements for Myself*) that Lucky was Godot. But in any case Vladimir and Estragon are trapped. There is nothing to force them to stay but there is no incentive to make them go. The only way out is death, and the only relief is night. They keep talking about suicide but they are incapable of taking any action or even of really wanting to. So in effect waiting for Godot is waiting for your life to be over, waiting for night to fall, waiting for the play to end.

The tensions of the normal play are constructed around the interaction of the characters and the ignorance of the audience about what is going to happen next. In *Waiting for Godot* they soon get to know that nothing is going to happen next and that there is no chance of any development of character through relationships. The characters are not characters in this sense. There are many passages where it could not matter less who says which line:

> ESTRAGON: They talk about their lives.
> VLADIMIR: To have lived is not enough for them.
> ESTRAGON: They have to talk about it.
> VLADIMIR: To be dead is not enough for them.
> ESTRAGON: It is not sufficient.
>   (*Silence.*)
> VLADIMIR: They make a noise like feathers.
> ESTRAGON: Like leaves.
> VLADIMIR: Like ashes.
> ESTRAGON: Like leaves.

But although it is not a play in the conventional sense, it is very much a play in the literal sense of the word "play." Having nothing to do with their time, Vladimir and Estragon are rather like children who have time to play games and have to play games to pass the time. "What shall we do now?" is in effect what they are always saying to each other, and some of their improvisations are very much like what children might think of to do. They play a game of being Pozzo and Lucky, they play at being very polite to each other, at abusing each other, at making it up, and they stagger about on one leg trying to look like trees. The audience is involved most directly when they look out in horror at the auditorium, but in fact the audience is involved in the game all the way through because Beckett is playing around with the fact of having actors on a stage playing parts, and playing around with the idea of a play. Instead of working to keep the audience guessing about what is going to happen next, he manages to give the impression of having written the play without himself knowing how he was going to go on. We feel that it is not only Vladimir and Estragon but also Beckett himself welcoming Pozzo and Lucky's second entrance as providing a diversion just at the right moment. There is an air of improvisation about the writing, and though the final script is one that allows no improvisation from the actors—it calls for great precision in performance—it has an engaging resemblance to the patter of a well-read conjurer. The tricks are simple ones, but the rapid changes of conversational gear are masterly. Anything that appears so spontaneous must have been well rehearsed. And for Beckett, of course, the rehearsal was *Mercier et Camier*.

But what about the tricks? The most important trick in the style and structure of *Waiting for Godot* is the old music-hall trick of protracted delay. No question can be answered and no action can be taken without a maximum of interlocution, incomprehension, and argument. You never go straight to a point if you can possibly miss it, evade it, or start a long discussion about a shortcut. Vladimir and Estragon ask Pozzo why Lucky doesn't put down the bags. Pozzo is delighted at having a question to answer, but it takes two pages of digression, repetition, incomprehension, cross-purpose dialogue and farcical preparations like spraying his throat before he actually answers it. Then a few minutes later, he wants to sit down, but he doesn't want to sit down until someone has asked him to sit; Estragon offers to ask him, he agrees, Estragon asks him, he refuses, pauses, and in an aside asks Estragon to ask him again; Estragon asks him again, and finally he sits.

There is also a great deal of vaudeville business with hats and boots and pratfalls. The bowler hats that all four characters wear belong to the tradition of Chaplin and Laurel and Hardy. Vladimir has a comic walk and a comic disability that makes him rush off to pee in the wings each time he is made to laugh, and Lucky has elaborate comic business with all the things he has to carry, dropping them, picking them up and putting them down. Although there is very little action, there are an enormous number of actions which the actors have to perform, and in which they are meticulously instructed by stage directions:

> (*Lucky weeps.*)
> ESTRAGON: He's crying.
> POZZO: Old dogs have more dignity.
> (*He proffers his handkerchief to Estragon.*)
> Comfort him, since you pity him.
> (*Estragon hesitates.*)
> Come on.
> (*Estragon takes the handkerchief.*)
> Wipe away his tears, he'll feel less forsaken.
> (*Estragon hesitates.*)
> VLADIMIR: Here, give it to me, I'll do it.
> (*Estragon refuses to give the handkerchief. Childish gestures.*)
> POZZO: Make haste, before he stops.
> (*Estragon approaches Lucky and makes to wipe his eyes. Lucky kicks him violently in the shins. Estragon drops the handkerchief, recoils, staggers about the stage howling with pain.*)
> Hanky!
> (*Lucky puts down bag and basket, picks up the handkerchief, gives it to Pozzo, goes back to his place, picks up bag and basket.*)

Another important trick is the way Beckett uses interruption. Almost everything in the play gets interrupted—Lucky's big speech, Estragon's story about the Englishman in the brothel, and Vladimir interrupts his own song about dogs digging a dog a tomb. But it is a song that circles back on itself, so, as with Lucky's speech, we welcome the interruption because we feel that otherwise it would have gone on forever.

All in all, though, the play's brisk rhythm depends less on the frequent interruptions than on the shortness of the speeches. There are very few long speeches, and these are judiciously placed at the points where they are most useful as a variation on the basic staccato. The average length of the speeches in *Waiting for Godot* must be less than in any other play ever written. Together with the rapid changes of topic, this builds up an impression of great speed. If Vladimir and Estragon are doing nothing, at least they are doing it fast.

The other couple, Pozzo and Lucky, are not "doing nothing" in the same sense. They are on a journey which appears to have a definite purpose. In Act One, Pozzo is intending to sell Lucky at the fair, and he keeps professing to be in a hurry, even if his behavior indicates the opposite.

ESTRAGON: Come, come, take a seat, I beseech you,
  you'll get pneumonia.
POZZO: You really think so?
ESTRAGON: Why, it's absolutely certain.
POZZO: You may be right.
  (*He sits down.*)
  Thank you, dear fellow.
  (*He consults his watch.*)

But I must really be getting along if I am to ob-
serve my schedule.

VLADIMIR: Time has stopped.

POZZO: (*cuddling his watch to his ear*): Don't you
believe it, sir, don't you believe it.

(*He puts his watch back in his pocket.*)
Whatever you like, but not that.

But his intention is forgotten or frustrated, and in
Act Two he is still with Lucky. The difference is that
now they are traveling in the opposite direction and
that now he is blind and Lucky is dumb. This has
been interpreted in various ways. Lucky has been
taken to be Pozzo's soul—"But for him all my
thoughts, all my feelings would have been of common
things." There was a stage in Pozzo's life when he
learned from Lucky, but this is over now; and having
exploited, abused, denied, and finally silenced the
spiritual side of his own nature until the very presence
of Lucky seems like a reproach, Pozzo, the materialist,
wants to be rid of him altogether. In the French version of the play, he is going to sell him in the "Marché
du Saint Sauveur." Certainly the overtone here must
be a deliberate one, but I believe it is always a mistake
to interpret Beckett by translating his images point for
point. If you impose a single "meaning" on a sequence, you may be hitting one nail too far in at the
cost of dislodging several others. In this particular
case the body-soul interpretation is illuminating up to
a point, and it fits beautifully with Pozzo's line

One journeys all alone . . . and never a soul in
sight.

But it tends to obscure the points about the Pozzo-
Lucky relationship which refer more obviously, but no

less meaningfully, to the mutual need of the master and the slave.

He imagines that when I see how well he carries I'll be tempted to keep him on in that capacity.

And if Pozzo's analysis of Lucky's behavior is accurate, Lucky too is doing something which has a purpose, however ludicrous. The very fact that it is made so ludicrous can be taken, among other things, as an indication of Beckett's contempt for the ambition to better one's position in the world of business and society.

The only progress that interests Beckett is not upwards and outwards but inwards and downwards. This is the kind of progress that the heroes of his novels make, and this is what he believes the artist should do.

The only possible spiritual development is in the sense of depth. The artistic tendency is not expansive, but a contraction. And art is the apotheosis of solitude. There is no communication because there are no vehicles of communication. Even on the rare occasions when word and gesture happen to be valid expressions of personality, they lose their significance on their passage through the cataract of the personality that is opposed to them. Either we speak and act for ourselves—in which case speech and action are distorted and emptied of their meaning by an intelligence that is not ours, or else we speak and act for others—in which case we speak and act a lie.

This attitude leads immediately to a rejection of realism. He warmly embraces Proust's contempt for the literature that "describes," for the realists and naturalists worshipping the offal of experience, prostrate before the epidermis and the swift epilepsy, and content to transcribe the surface, the façade, behind which the Idea is prisoner.

In fact, Proust's pictures of contemporary Paris society are very much more realistic than you would gather from reading Beckett's book about him, but what is more interesting is the consistency with which Beckett has subsequently stuck by the principles he laid down for the artist thirty-five years ago.

The only fertile research is excavatory, immersive, a contraction of the spirit, a descent. The artist is active, but negatively, shrinking from the nullity of extracircumferential phenomena, drawn into the core of the eddy.

In this light, the pattern of "doing nothing" takes on a rather different significance. All Beckett's heroes have been subject to drives which, like his ideal artist's drives, tend to isolate them from the world of relationships and activity. His first hero, Belacqua, who appears in both the stories *The Dream of Fair to Middling Women* and *More Pricks than Kicks* was named after the indolent Florentine lutemaker in Dante's Ante-purgatory who said, "It is by sitting and resting that the soul grows wise." It is the ambition of Beckett's Belacqua

to break not so much the flow of people and things to him as the ebb of him to people and

things. It was his instinct to make himself captive . . .

And the object of his self-imposed captivity is to free
his mind from the preoccupations with the world and
everyday living so that it can turn in on itself.

> In the umbra, the tunnel, when the mind went
> wombtomb, then it was real thought and real liv-
> ing, living thought. Thought not skivvying for liv-
> ing nor living chivvying thought up to the six-and-
> eightpenny conviction, but live cerebration that
> drew no wages and emptied no slops.

Beckett's next hero, Murphy, has the same instinct
as Belacqua to make himself captive, and his favorite
indulgence is to lock the door of his room and tie
himself naked to a rocking chair. Like Belacqua, he is
heavily involved in personal relationships when we
first meet him, but we see him steadily withdrawing
into isolation. He is attracted to the prostitute who is
in love with him, but

> the part of him that he hated craved for Celia, the
> part that he loved shrivelled up at the thought of
> her.

So rather than go on living with her, he chooses the
refuge and relative peace of a menial, living-in job in
an asylum. Murphy's mind is described as "a hollow
sphere, hermetically closed to the universe" and its
recoil from contact with the "big blooming buzzing
confusion" of external reality develops into an almost

mystical pursuit of positive gratifications in negative qualities.

> Murphy began to see nothing, that colourlessness which is such a rare postnatal treat, being the absence (to abuse a nice distinction) not of *percipere* but of *percipi*. His other senses also found themselves at peace, an unexpected pleasure. Not the numb peace of their own suspension, but the positive peace that comes when the somethings give way, or perhaps simply add up, to the Nothing, than which in the guffaw of the Abderite naught is more real. Time did not cease, that would be asking too much, but the wheel of rounds and pauses did, as Murphy with his head among the armies continued to suck in, through all the posterns of his withered soul, the accident-less One-and-Only, conveniently called Nothing. Then this also vanished, or perhaps simply came asunder, in the familiar variety of stenches, asperities, ear-splitters and eye-closers, and Murphy saw that Mr. Endon was missing.

In this rather wilfully erudite prose, the narrative situation (Murphy playing chess with Mr. Endon,* one of the inmates of the asylum) almost vanishes in the delighted description of Murphy's progress from taking delight in nothing to taking delight in Nothing. The point is a very important one but the rather heavy-handed parody of the scholastic manner gets in the way of what is being said. There is a good deal of the same kind of joke in *Waiting for Godot*, when Vladimir and Estragon get pedantic, but Beckett's touch by then has become very much lighter.

---

* In Greek, Endon means "within."

In *Watt*, the whole episode at the house of Mr. Knott (whose very name invokes the negative) can be seen as an encounter with Nothingness. The servant Arsène, who is leaving as Watt arrives, describes how

> having oscillated all his life between the torments of a superficial loitering and the horrors of disinterested endeavour, he finds himself at last in a situation where to do nothing exclusively would be an act of the highest value, and significance.

While working for Mr. Knott, he finds that he is working

> also, and indeed chiefly, for himself, that he may abide, as he is, where he is, and that where he is may abide about him, as it is. Unable to resist these intenerating considerations, his regrets, lively at first, melt at last, melt quite away and pass over, softly, into the celebrated conviction that all is well, or at least for the best. His indignation undergoes a similar reduction, and calm and glad at last he goes about his work, calm and glad he peels the potato and empties the nightstool, calm and glad he witnesses and is witnessed. For a time.

The feeling of well-being does not last, however, as Watt himself is later to find. All the time that he's employed as a servant on the ground floor, he hardly sees Mr. Knott. The one time they meet on the lawn he does not see his face and "little by little Watt abandoned all hope, all fear, of ever seeing Mr. Knott face to face." When, eventually, he moves up to the first floor, where he is in contact with Mr. Knott all the time, he still isn't very much the wiser. For, to him, Mr. Knott seems to change in appearance from one day to the next, and his effect is to dim and dull everything around him.

> For except, one, not to need, and two, a witness of his not needing, Knott needed nothing, as far as Watt could see.

This stress on witnessing and needing to be witnessed is very interesting. Knott is Nothing, but Nothing needs to exist and he needs two servants, one of which, on the upper floor, will witness him, so that he can be sure of his own existence. This situation is repeated almost exactly in *Godot* in the scene where Vladimir talks to the little boy, Godot's messenger, while Estragon is asleep. It is as if Godot is himself afraid of not existing and needs the reassurance of the two tramps' continuing belief in him. But he is also, like Knott, a Nothing figure and this is the only extent to which his existence is real. Nothing is more real than nothing. The paradox is very much on the lines of Hamm's complaint, in *Endgame*, about God: "The bastard he doesn't exist."

Godot cannot finally be equated either with the "Other" of the existentialists or with God, but together with other hints, the stress on witnessing and being witnessed and the frequent references to the Bible do push us in the direction of both equations. Lucky's speech starts off by postulating "the existence as uttered forth in the public works of Puncher and Wattmann of a personal God quaquaquaqua with white beard quaquaquaqua outside time without extension."

At the end of Act Two, Vladimir asks the boy what Godot looks like.

> VLADIMIR (*softly*): Has he a beard, Mr. Godot?
> BOY: Yes, sir.
> VLADIMIR: Fair or . . . (*he hesitates*) . . . or black?
> BOY: I think it's white, sir.
>   *Silence*
> VLADIMIR: Christ have mercy on us!
>   *Silence*
> BOY: What am I to say to Mr. Godot, sir?
> VLADIMIR: Tell him . . . (*he hesitates*) . . . tell him you saw me and that . . . (*he hesitates*) . . . that you saw me.

And when Estragon wakes up, after the boy has gone, and asks Vladimir what would happen if they dropped Godot, the answer is, "He'd punish us." Yet they are very vague about what is required of them by Godot, just as Moran, the agent in *Molloy*, is vague about Youdi, his boss, whom he has never seen. He resents him, but obeys him, or at least he starts off with the intention of obeying, though later he runs into difficulties, which include the difficulty of remembering what the orders were, just as the tramps in *Godot* are very vague by the time the action starts of what their arrangements with Godot were. They are uncertain what exactly they asked him to do for them and they cannot remember what his reply was, only that it was noncommittal. They are not sure that they are waiting in the right place, by the right tree, and neither of them knows which day of the week it is, so it may not be the right day.

This is another feature of *Waiting for Godot* which is very puzzling unless you are familiar with the rest of Beckett's work—the extraordinary difficulty everyone has in remembering anything. Neither of the tramps can remember where they were yesterday and Estragon isn't sure whether the people who have just beaten him are the same lot that usually do. In Act Two he has forgotten that they tried to hang themselves in Act One, and it is only when Vladimir reminds him about Pozzo and Lucky that he can remember anything except being kicked. Pozzo too turns out to have forgotten the meeting on the previous day. If it weren't for the stage direction which tells us that Act Two is a day later, we'd assume that much more time had elapsed between the two acts, especially when we find that Pozzo has forgotten when he went blind and when Lucky went dumb. And he gets very angry when questioned about it.

> Have you not done tormenting me with your accursed time? It's abominable. When! When! One day, is that not enough for you, one day like any other day, one day he went dumb, one day I went blind, one day we'll go deaf, one day we were born, one day we'll die, the same day, the same second, is that not enough for you?

Pozzo's indifference about time is rivaled only by Estragon's indifference about place. For him, everywhere is the same as everywhere else, and like Pozzo, he is liable to a sudden burst of anger when questioned.

> VLADIMIR: Do you not recognize the place?
> ESTRAGON: Recognize! What is there to recognize? All my lousy life I've crawled about in the mud! And you talk to me about scenery! (*Looking*

wildly about him.) Look at this muckheap! I've never stirred from it!

The divisions of time and place are arbitrary and irrelevant. It is all a void, so it could not matter less what artificial categorizations are imposed on it.

VLADIMIR: And where were we yesterday evening according to you?
ESTRAGON: How do I know? In another compartment. There's no lack of void.

To understand this attitude fully, you have to turn back once again to the book on Proust. There is an illuminating passage where Beckett compares what Proust called "involuntary memory" with "voluntary memory." The famous incident of the madeleine is an example of involuntary memory—a sense experience sets up a train of associations in the mind; they bring the past flooding back as it actually was, and not as you would think it was if you tried to recall it. The real past is the past which includes you as you then were and not just the objects and incidents that you think you remember—pinned down and static. Voluntary memory is

the uniform memory of intelligence; and it can be relied on to reproduce for our gratified inspection those impressions of the past that were consciously and intelligently formed. It has no interest in the mysterious element of inattention that colours our most commonplace experiences. It presents the past in monochrome. The images it chooses are as arbitrary as those chosen by imagination, and are equally remote from reality.

Memory is also affected by the fact that the perceiving mind is itself not quite the same from one day to the next.

There is no escape from yesterday because yesterday has deformed us, or been deformed by us. The mood is of no importance. Deformation has taken place. Yesterday is not a milestone that has been passed, but a daystone on the beaten track of the years, and irremediably part of us, within us, heavy and dangerous. We are not merely more weary because of yesterday, we are other, no longer what we were before the calamity of yesterday. A calamitous day, but calamitous not necessarily in content. The good or evil disposition of the object has neither reality nor significance. The immediate joys and sorrows of the body and the intelligence are so many superfoetations. Such as it was, it has been assimilated to the only world that has reality and significance, the world of our own latent consciousness, and its cosmography has suffered a dislocation. So that we are rather in the position of Tantalus, with this difference, that we allow ourselves to be tantalized. And possibly the *perpetuum mobile* of our disillusions is subject to more variety. The aspirations of yesterday were valid for yesterday's ego, not for today's. We are disappointed at the nullity of what we are pleased to call attainment. But what is attainment? The identification of the subject with the object of his desire. The subject has died—and perhaps many times—on the way. For subject B to be disappointed by the banality of an object chosen by subject A is as illogical as to expect one's hunger to be dissipated by the spectacle of Uncle eating his dinner.

Beckett's rejection of naturalism in art follows logically from his skepticism about the perceiving mind. He sees it as an instrument incapable of registering accurately the reality that confronts it. There is no

> direct and purely experimental contact possible between subject and object, because they are automatically separated by the subject's consciousness of perception, and the object loses its purity and becomes a mere intellectual pretext or motive.

The intelligence is always censoring new experiences and rejecting as illogical and insignificant all the elements that do not fit with its preconceived ideas. The censoring process is necessary because reality would be intolerable for us if we had to face it as it really is. The reality we see is just a projection of our consciousness. We are habitually adapting, falsifying, and faking evidence in order to adjust the human organism to the conditions of its existence.

If you genuinely believe that what normally passes for reality is actually so much fiction, the most real element in the fiction you write will be the uncertainty. In the incident of the piano tuners, Watt is not uncertain about what happened or about whether it happened, but about what it really was that happened, what it amounts to. If the matter could have been settled at the time, he would not need to be thinking about it now, but for Beckett, and his characters, this kind of uncertainty about past events, irrespective of whether they are in the remote past or the immediate past, keeps dragging them into the present. To be sure of the reality of your own existence, you need to be sure of what has happened to you. Which is impossible without an independent witness. This is why Vladimir and Estragon spend so much time arguing about what happened yesterday. And if you cannot be certain about yesterday's events, how can you be certain of today's? Are they really happening or is it all in the mind?

> Was I sleeping, while the others suffered? Am I sleeping now? Tomorrow, when I wake, or think I do, what shall I say of today? That with Estragon, my friend, at this place, until the fall of night, I waited for Godot? That Pozzo passed, with his carrier, and talked to us? Probably. But in all that what truth will there be? (*Estragon, having struggled with his boots in vain, is dozing off again. Vladimir stares at him.*) He'll know nothing. He'll tell me about the blows he received and I'll give him a carrot. (*Pause.*) Astride of a grave and a difficult birth. Down in the hole, lingeringly, the grave-digger puts on the forceps. We have time to grow old. The air is full of our cries. (*He listens.*) But habit is a great deadener. (*He looks again at Estragon.*) At me too someone is looking, of me too someone is saying, He is sleeping, he knows nothing, let him sleep on. (*Pause.*) I can't go on! (*Pause.*) What have I said?

The need for a witness from outside is the strongest reason of all for wanting Godot to be real.

In this passage, it is not just the past but also the

future that gets dragged into Vladimir's questioning awareness of the present. And this is a small and early example of what later becomes an important tendency in Beckett—to merge all the tenses into a continuous present. The immediate experience is shown to be the same as past experiences, and memories of the past are constantly recurring in the present. In *Krapp's Last Tape*, Krapp's present consists entirely of playing recordings made in the past and making recordings for the future, while the characters in *Play* are trapped in a still less naturalistic kind of present, made up of gabbled fragments of their past, and their future will be the same. There is no development in Beckett's plays because, according to him, development is impossible. Any indications of it are illusory. This is why the total action of his plays goes no farther than the basic situation. Both action and situation can be summed up in the same present participle: two tramps waiting for a Messiah; a master and his servant waiting for the end; an old man playing magnetic tapes; a fifty-year-old woman talking, half-buried in sand; and three ex-lovers talking, imprisoned in urns.

Apart from occasional children, all Beckett's characters are either old or very old. Except in the early novels and short stories, there is hardly a single adolescent or young or middle-aged adult in the whole of his work. Youth is represented only by memories of a girl on a boat, or of the time when one wasn't too decrepit to be refused admission to the Eiffel Tower. And the memory of past hopefulness is severely framed by the hopelessness of the present.

The preoccupation with time is constant—it would be hard to count the number of times that the word "time" is mentioned in *Waiting for Godot*. The pursuit of the extra-temporal has become less compulsive since *Murphy* and *Watt*, but it is still present in *Waiting for Godot*. In fact that is exactly what *Waiting for Godot* is, a humorous lament for the failure of the finite self to make contact with the Other, the witness that is outside space and time.

You could say with equal truth that all Beckett's plays are about the passage of time or that they're about the refusal of time to pass. When Vladimir and Estragon say that time has stopped, this doesn't just mean that it is passing slowly. There is a sense in which it does stop during the play. We see Pozzo consult his watch four times during his first scene, and at the end of the scene he tries hard to find it, fumbling in his pockets and searching on the ground, all in vain, deciding finally that he must have left it back at the manor. One commentator has suggested that it is through meeting Vladimir and Estragon that Pozzo loses his contact with time. Certainly his attitude to it changes during the course of the action. It is a big jump from his initial involvement with time to his indifference to it in Act Two. But it doesn't matter whether you attribute this to the influence of Vladimir and Estragon, the loss of his watch, or the loss of his sight. In any case, both losses are symbolical of entering a world in which time and space do not have their normal significance. The tree grows four or five leaves overnight and the events of five minutes ago are as hard to remember as the remote past. We feel as though we are halfway towards being outside time altogether, and we almost despair, with Vladimir and Estragon, of night ever falling.

The three constant, contradictory complaints in

Beckett's work are that time doesn't pass at all but stays around us, like a continuum, that it passes too slowly, and that too much of it passes. It is because so much of it has gone by for them that so many of his characters have become so decrepit, lost so many limbs and faculties. Molloy and Moran both go on deteriorating rapidly in the course of the novel, and Malone is often uncertain about whether he is already dead, an uncertainty that he shares with the nameless, perhaps bodiless narrative voices in *Textes pour rien* and *The Unnamable*. Bom, in *How It Is*, and the characters in *Play* are all situated somewhere outside temporal existence.

In its basic statements, *Waiting for Godot* is no less serious than these other works, but it is much more buoyantly ambiguous in its style, leaving audiences free to take it on whichever level they choose. When Vladimir and Estragon discuss the two thieves and the prospects of salvation, one possible reaction is "How ridiculous! Two tramps having a theological discussion!" And we can leave it at that. And when they talk about hanging themselves, we laugh at the clowning. Pozzo takes himself seriously, but Vladimir and Estragon mock themselves incessantly, and their language is both a parody of academic argument and a self-parody.

> ESTRAGON: Can you not stay still?
> VLADIMIR: I'm cold.
> ESTRAGON: We came too early.
> VLADIMIR: It's always at nightfall.
> ESTRAGON: But night doesn't fall.
> VLADIMIR: It'll fall all of a sudden, like yesterday.
> ESTRAGON: Then it'll be night.
> VLADIMIR: And we can go.

ESTRAGON: Then it'll be day again. (*Pause. Despairing.*) What'll we do! What'll we do!
VLADIMIR: (*halting, violently*): Will you stop whining! I've had about my bellyful of your lamentations!

This is at once literary and colloquial, and it accommodates both great precision and great vagueness. But it is splendidly surefooted. It is exactly what it sets out to be and gives all its subject matter just the focus that Beckett intends. It is playful language, language that plays with itself as language, but for all its mockery, it also expresses quite a positive tenderness between Vladimir and Estragon, highlighting the quasi-marital bickering satirically but sensitively.

VLADIMIR: (*joyous*): There you are again . . . (*indifferently.*) There we are again . . . (*gloomy.*) There I am again.
ESTRAGON: You see, you feel worse when I'm with you. I feel better alone, too.
VLADIMIR (*piqued*): Then why do you come crawling back?
ESTRAGON: *I* don't know.
VLADIMIR: No, but I do. It's because you don't know how to take care of yourself. I wouldn't have let them beat you.
ESTRAGON: You couldn't have stopped them.
VLADIMIR: Why not?
ESTRAGON: There were ten of them.
VLADIMIR: No, I mean before they beat you. I would have stopped you from doing whatever it was you were doing.

With all the provocative gaps that there are in *Waiting for Godot* between the matter and the manner, between the half-statements and the half-meanings, it invites so much comment that it is easy to leave the most important point of all relatively unstressed—that it is consistently so very funny. In production, of course, there's a danger of getting bogged down in portentousness and letting the effervescence go out of the dialogue if the pace is too slow. But the script provides the possibility of an evening in the theater which is never less than entertaining and often very much more.

"There I'll be, in the old refuge, alone against the silence and . . . the stillness." George Devine as Hamm in *Endgame* at the Royal Court.
DAVID SIM

Opposite: Nicol Williamson, right, as Vladimir and Alfred Lynch as Estragon in a British production of *Waiting for Godot* at the Royal Court Theatre.
DOMINIC

Hume Cronyn in *Krapp's Last Tape*. The play was one of four given during a 1972 Beckett Festival at the Forum Theater of the Lincoln Center.

MARTHA SWOPE

Below: Hume Cronyn as Willie and Jessica Tandy as Winnie in the Forum Theater production of *Happy Days*. Though she is buried in sand, Winnie's habitual optimism survives.

MARTHA SWOPE

Opposite: The pantomime *Act Without Words I*, starring Hume Cronyn, was part of the festival of Beckett plays directed by Alan Schneider at the Forum.

MARTHA SWOPE

Jack MacGowran in the 1966 BBC-2 production of *Eh, Joe*. The interior monologue accompanying the action is in a woman's voice.

BBC

Endgame

Endgame is not as good a play as *Waiting for Godot*. It starts off without the advantage that *Godot* shares with *Krapp's Last Tape* of having a central image which brilliantly crystallizes the total feeling of the play. *Endgame* gives a kind of definition to its title but "Endgame" never takes on anything like as clear a meaning as "Waiting for Godot." We get a strong enough feeling that Hamm's world is approaching its end, but the game is much less definite than the various games in *Waiting for Godot* and the whole play is much less playful. Instead of leaving the audience free to take its jokes as nothing more than jokes, *Endgame* is a much less relaxed piece of writing that insists on being taken seriously as a statement about the human condition.

Of course, there is still a certain amount of comedy, and there is still the same ratio of three characters who could be described as clowns to one who could not. But Hamm dictates the overall tone of *Endgame* in a way that Pozzo never did, even in the scenes that he dominated. And above all we miss the balance that was achieved in the Vladimir–Estragon relationship, with each of them beautifully deflating the other.

38

VLADIMIR: We are not saints, but we have kept our appointment. How many people can boast as much?
ESTRAGON: Billions.

Sometimes Clov's lines have a similar effect on Hamm, but they are fighting at very different weights and Beckett often has to resort to monologues in which Hamm deflates himself.

No doubt. Formerly. But now? (*Pause.*) My father? (*Pause.*) My mother? (*Pause.*) My . . . dog? (*Pause.*) Oh I am willing to believe they suffer as much as such creatures can suffer. But does that mean their sufferings equal mine? No doubt. (*Pause.*) No, all is a—(*he yawns*)—bso-lute, (*proudly*) the bigger a man is the fuller he is. (*Pause. Gloomily.*) And the emptier.

Altogether there is much less give-and-take in the dialogue than in *Waiting for Godot*, more dependence on long speeches, and very much less movement. Of the four characters, Hamm is confined to his armchair, Nagg and Nell are confined to bobbing up and down in their garbage cans, and Clov is the only character who can move about. The interdependence of Hamm and Clov is very much like that of Pozzo and Lucky in *Waiting for Godot*. Hamm cannot stand and Clov cannot sit. Hamm is the master and Clov is the slave. Hamm needs Clov to get him up, push him about in the armchair (which is on castors), and bring him food. Clov needs Hamm because only he knows the combination on the larder lock. Nagg and Nell also need Clov because he feeds them and changes the sand in their garbage cans.

The restriction of movement heightens the obvious interdependence of the characters, but it also limits the possibilities of knockabout comedy which was so important in *Waiting for Godot*. We get Clov rushing backwards and forwards, on and off, fetching whatever Hamm wants and appearing whenever Hamm whistles. He climbs up and down ladders, training his telescope on the world outside and reporting what he sees. He has business very similar to Lucky's, picking things up and putting them down in instant obedience to Hamm's orders, and there is the comedy act with the homemade dog. Hamm throws it aside when it wets him. But although Beckett is quite inventive within the limits that he sets himself, very little can be invented within such incredibly narrow limits.

It is especially when we get echoes of *Waiting for Godot* that we realize how much more labored the comedy here is. There is the same kind of attempt to involve the audience. Pointing his telescope at them, Clov says:

> I see . . . a multitude . . . in transports . . . of joy.
> (*Pause.*) That's what I call a magnifier.

There are similar references to the fact of its being a play.

> CLOV: What is there to keep me here?
> HAMM: The dialogue.

There is an attempt at the same use of a refrain:

> HAMM: What's happening?
> CLOV: Something is taking its course.

But this is less effective than the tramps' refrain of
"Let's go." "We can't." "Why not?" "We're waiting for
Godot." "Ah." Altogether the build-up of internal
echoes in *Endgame* achieves nothing like the same resonance that it did in *Waiting for Godot*. And there's
even another joke about urinating. But whereas it's
funny when Vladimir has to rush off into the wings
each time he is made to laugh, it is not very funny
when Hamm says he is having a pee on stage.

The play is ambiguous about whether Clov is
Hamm's son, but what matters is that this is another
relationship between a blind master and a willing
slave. Hamm's tone is often reminiscent of Pozzo's.

> Can there be misery—(*he yawns*)—loftier than
> mine?

And there is the same insistence that relations between them used to be better than they are now.

> HAMM: Why do you stay with me?
> CLOV: Why do you keep me?
> HAMM: There's no one else.
> CLOV: There's nowhere else.
>   (*Pause.*)
> HAMM: You're leaving me all the same.
> CLOV: I'm trying.
> HAMM: You don't love me.
> CLOV: No.
> HAMM: You loved me once.
> CLOV: Once!
> HAMM: I've made you suffer too much. (*Pause.*)
>   Haven't I?
> CLOV: It's not that.

> HAMM (*shocked*): I haven't made you suffer too
> much?
> CLOV: Yes!

But again this is much more clumsily explicit than
anything in *Waiting for Godot*.

There is the same kind of reference to the feeling
which is induced by the action (or by the inaction)
that time is passing slowly. But the boredom is
equated much less subtly with boredom with life as a
whole.

> HAMM: Have you not had enough?
> CLOV: Yes! (*Pause.*) Of what?
> HAMM: Of this . . . this . . . thing.
> CLOV: I always had. (*Pause.*) Not you?
> HAMM (*gloomily*): Then there's no reason for it
> to change.
> CLOV: It may end. (*Pause.*) All life long the same
> questions, the same answers.

And again, half an hour later.

> HAMM: Do you not think this has gone on long
> enough?
> CLOV: Yes! (*Pause.*) What?
> HAMM: This . . . this . . . thing.
> CLOV: I've always thought so. (*Pause.*) You not?
> HAMM (*gloomily*): Then it's a day like any other.
> CLOV: As long as it lasts. (*Pause.*) All life long the
> same inanities.

Of course it's part of Beckett's point that these characters are very half-hearted in playing the game at all.
Hamm yawns in the middle of his first line, "Me—to
play!" Though Beckett wants their improvisations to

seem labored, the effect is still too close to labored writing.

But then, nothing in *Endgame* falls into perspective and it is chiefly this that makes the play so hard to take. Its ambiguities stick in the throat. Hamm's world is coming to an end, but is his world intended to be our world? Where is it located in relation to ours? In *Waiting for Godot* there was very little to orient us in relation to external reality. We were already on the way towards being outside space and time. We only had one tree to represent Nature and a vague impression of surrounding countryside. But in *Endgame* Nature is dead or dying. The only evidence of it is that we lose our hair, our teeth, our bloom, our ideals. Nagg is crying, therefore he is still alive. We are situated inside a room which has only the barest resemblance to a room anyone could live in. There is no furniture, except for Hamm's armchair and there are two garbage cans inside the room. Of the two curtained windows in the back wall, which are too high to be reached without climbing a ladder, one looks out on the land and the other on the water, but nothing is to be seen through either. There is also a picture hanging with its face to the wall.

The whole scene has been taken as a stage picture of life inside the brain, with the two windows as eyes and Clov's business of drawing back the curtains and taking the dust sheet off Hamm standing for waking up in the morning. The garbage cans would then be a very disenchanted reference to Proust's vases—containing useless memories of the past. Martin Esslin, in his *Theatre of the Absurd*, goes on to ask whether Clov can be equated with "the intellect, bound to serve the emotions, instincts, and appetites, and trying to free himself from such disorderly and tyrannical masters, yet doomed to die when its connection with the animal side of the personality is severed." But like all the other ingenious equations that commentators on Beckett have suggested,* this doesn't work for more than some aspects of the Hamm–Clov relationship. There are also several passages that make us think of Hamm as a sort of Godot, whose help was needed and who now rather regrets that he was always absent.

> All those I might have helped. (*Pause.*) Helped! (*Pause.*) Saved. (*Pause.*) Saved! (*Pause.*) The place was crawling with them!

You could find just as much justification in the text for equating him with an absent God as for equating him with the "emotions, instincts, and appetites." At one time Clov used to go around inspecting Hamm's paupers, but Hamm never went himself.

> HAMM: I was never there.
> CLOV: Lucky for you. (*He looks out of window.*)
> HAMM: Absent, always. It all happened without me. I don't know what's happened. (*Pause.*) Do you know what's happened?

And he rejected all the suppliants who came to him, refusing what he could have given them, corn from

* There's a good example in Vivian Mercier's review of *Molloy* in *The New Statesman and Nation*, equating Molloy with the id and Moran with the ego. Molloy, like the id, has no sense of time and nothing but instinctual drives which contradict each other without neutralizing each other, while Moran, hounded by the superego, is full of anxiety and guilt.

his granaries and oil for their lamps. A Mother Pegg is referred to as having "died of darkness" as a result.

In so far as he is God, he is not a creator but a destroyer. He wants the end to come. Any survival of life around him—a rat, a flea, a child—is a threat to him, and he orders Clov to annihilate it. In a sense he is like Mr. Knott, a personification of the void. Underneath his dark glasses, the eyes have gone all white, and seeing nothing, he can see Nothingness. The vision is expressed savagely in the speech in which he warns Clov that he will come more and more to resemble him, unable to move, unable to see.

One day you'll be blind, like me. You'll be sitting there, a speck in the void, in the dark, for ever, like me. (*Pause.*) One day you'll say to yourself, I'm tired, I'll sit down, and you'll go and sit down. Then you'll say, I'm hungry, I'll get up and get something to eat. But you won't get up. You'll say, I shouldn't have sat down, but since I have I'll sit on a little longer, then I'll get up and get something to eat. But you won't get up and you won't get anything to eat. (*Pause.*) You'll look at the wall a while, then you'll say, I'll close my eyes, perhaps have a little sleep, after that I'll feel better, and you'll close them. And when you open them again there'll be no wall any more. (*Pause.*) Infinite emptiness will be all around you, all the resurrected dead of all the ages wouldn't fill it, and there you'll be like a little bit of grit in the middle of the steppe. (*Pause.*) Yes, one day, you'll know what it is, you'll be like me, except that you won't have anyone with you, because you won't have had pity on anyone and because there won't be anyone left to have pity on.

Describing the difference between the later novels and *Murphy*, Hugh Kenner said: "To write it he simply evaded the madness in himself. To write the latter books he confronted this madness." *Endgame* is certainly a play in which he confronts the madness. Hamm has one speech which makes a gesture towards getting it into focus:

> I once knew a madman who thought the end of the world had come. He was a painter—and engraver. I had a great fondness for him. I used to go and see him, in the asylum. I'd take him by the hand and drag him to the window. Look! There! All that rising corn! And there! Look! The sails of the herring fleet! All that loveliness! (*Pause.*) He'd snatch away his hand and go back into his corner. Appalled. All he had seen was ashes. (*Pause.*) He alone had been spared. (*Pause.*) Forgotten. (*Pause.*) It appears the case is . . . was not so . . . so unusual.

There may be only one window in the room in the asylum, but from it you can see the land and the water as you can from the two windows in Hamm's room. The madman sees only ashes, Clov reports "nothing" and "zero" when he looks out of the windows. But is Hamm just a madman who thinks the end of the world has come and Clov just a function of his madness? The speech seems to be aimed at providing a microcosm for the whole play, and there are some other hints which reinforce the invitation it gives us to dismiss Hamm's vision as insane. There is the appearance of the small boy at the end of the play after we'd been led to believe that there was no life "outside of here." Hamm had mentioned the possibility that there was life elsewhere.

> Here we're down a hole. But beyond the hills? Eh? Perhaps it's still green. Eh?

This is rather reminiscent of a passage in *Malone Dies*.

> And indeed the silence at times is such that the earth seems uninhabited. That is what comes of the taste for generalization. You have only to hear nothing for a few days, in your hole, nothing but the sounds of things, and you begin to fancy yourself the last of human kind.

But the whole tendency of *Endgame* supports the feeling that there is nothing green and nothing alive outside. We accept the evidence indicating that this is the end. It won't rain. There are no more bicycles. There's no more pap. There is no more Nature. I see my light dying. The seeds *will* never sprout. Nagg has lost his tooth. The doctor is dead. The time is the same as usual. The weather is the same as usual. The light is sunk. Everything is gray. How could anyone's light be on? There are no more sugarplums. Our revels now are ended. There is no more tide. There are no more navigators. There are no more rugs. There is no more painkiller. This is the end of the game, the game of the end, and Hamm's last move is to cover his face with the handkerchief, lowering his arm to the armrests and remaining motionless. In fact Clov is still standing there watching, but Hamm believes that he has gone and that there is no one left to witness him. If he neither sees nor is seen, then he doesn't exist.

In Dr. Milton Rokeach's book *The Three Christs of Ypsilanti,* we are given a detailed account of the attitudes and behavior of three paranoid schizophrenics who each believe that they are God. One of them becomes emotionally involved with a research assistant and defends himself against his own feelings towards her, first by sitting at meetings with his eyes shut and later on by making a dark green cellophane blindfold for himself, through which he can hardly see. He wears it all the time "for metaphysical reasons," he says. For a time he wears earplugs too, behaving towards the woman as if she did not exist, and sometimes withdrawing altogether from all social contact. "I go into a realm where it is more peaceful." Often his utterances border on poetic statement. Confronted with a handwritten script of his own, he repudiates it as prompted by the insanity of God, and claiming that he is "Dr. R. I. Dung, a reincarnation of Jesus Christ," he talks about a Dung Chapel in the Sahara Desert where he intends to live for the next five to seven years. Recoiling from sex, he says "It's better to live alone, relating to positive nothingness." He comes to see himself as a hermaphrodite and claims that it's the innate characteristic of the "morphodite," as he calls it, to kill its parents and to "born itself." His "femaleity" wants "positive idealed love without attachment." "Nobody offered it to me so my maleity offered it and I married myself." It's difficult to relate to other people because their presence and their remarks may be threats to the schizophrenic's belief in his own delusions. A typical defense is to deny that the others are alive. The need to withdraw is very much like that of another schizophrenic whose "poem" is quoted by Dr. Rokeach.

Yes, I want the cave,
There, I know where I am.
I can grope, in the dark,
   and feel the cave walls.
And the people, there, know I'm there,
   and they step on me, by mistake—
I think, I hope.
But, outside—
Where am I?

The correspondence between this cave and Hamm's hole are obvious enough, and Hamm has a number of traits which can be seen as schizophrenic. The question even arises of whether he has chosen immobility and chosen not to see. Some of his guilt feelings center on his never having wanted to go out to help his paupers, and if the speech in which he predicts blindness and immobility for Clov is based, as it seems to be, on his own experience, his paralysis and his blindness are seen to be within a province controlled at least partly by his own willpower. Having gone that far, it is only one step farther to start thinking in terms of schizophrenia about his consignment of his parents to garbage cans, his asexuality, his hints of godlike powers, his longing for the end, his cultivation of a relationship with absolute nothingness, and his belief that everyone else is dead. But if all this is madness, it is not peculiar to Hamm but pervasive to the whole play. Apart from the one speech about the madman who looks at herring fleets and sees ashes, and the one hint that there may be life beyond the hills, there is no chink to let any light into the dark chamber of Hamm's blind vision, which is supported by Clov's reports of "zero" and "nothing."

Whether or not you accept the view that the play is

a monodrama, with the whole action lodged in the interior of one brain, it is certainly a solipsist play and the solipsism remains intact even after the surprising and enigmatic appearance of the child at the end. It is written from inside the solipsism and once you enter a solipsist world there is no way of measuring the temperature of the madness. Any thermometer you have brought with you from the world outside is valueless. There are no norms. The question of how far Beckett wants us to share Hamm's view of the world and the human condition is unanswerable.

And yet the question is not altogether to be avoided. As Jan Kott has emphasized,* speaking of Beckett's "Theatrum mundi," the new "grotesque" deals with the same problems, conflicts and themes as tragedy— "human fate, the meaning of existence, freedom and inevitability, the discrepancy between the absolute and the fragile human order."

> In a tragic and grotesque world, situations are imposed, compulsory and inescapable. Freedom of choice and decision are part of this compulsory situation, in which both the tragic hero and the grotesque actor must always lose their struggle against the absolute. The downfall of the tragic hero is a confirmation and recognition of the absolute; whereas the downfall of the grotesque actor means mockery of the absolute and its desecration.

In their final speeches, both Hamm and Clov refer

---

* In his *Shakespeare Our Contemporary* in the chapter on "King Lear, or Endgame."

to an undefined third person plural or some power
outside themselves.

> I say to myself—sometimes, Clov, you must learn
> to suffer better than that if you want them to
> weary of punishing you—one day. I say to myself
> —sometimes, Clov, you must be there better than
> that if you want them to let you go—one day. But
> I feel too old, and too far, to form new habits.
> Good, it'll never end, I'll never go.

Hamm is less explicit in postulating the existence of
powers that control the circumstances of material existence, but the assumption is still there.

> You prayed—(*Pause. He corrects himself.*) You
> CRIED for night; it comes—(*Pause. He corrects
> himself.*) It FALLS: now cry in darkness.

This is not a very objective or realistic way of qualify-
ing the play's solipsism, but if there is belief in a
punitive exterior force that makes us exist, makes us
suffer, and makes us wait impatiently for nightfall or
for the end, then there is a belief in something real
outside the self.

I do not want to make more than a brief and tenta-
tive skirmish into the biographical, but it would be
wrong to overlook the encounter with failing eyesight
that Beckett had through his friendship with James
Joyce. He was never Joyce's secretary (though he is
often said to have been), but he did help Joyce by
reading to him. It would be interesting to know
whether Joyce's compulsive crowding of as much living material as he could get from twenty-four hours of
Dublin life into a single novel was partly a response to

the knowledge that his eyesight was failing. The Argentinian novelist Jorge Luis Borges, who also went blind, reacted very differently. "Why take 500 pages to develop an idea whose oral demonstration fits into a few minutes?" Beckett, who has many affinities with Borges, also inclines towards reductionism. His novels have progressively excluded more and more of the inessential, becoming ever more austere in their definitions of the boundaries of the essential, while his plays have progressively rejected more and more of the visual possibilities that the medium of theater offers. And *Endgame* handles the subject of blindness explicitly enough to raise the question of whether the personal fear of failing sight may partly account for the failure to focus the play's solipsism more clearly. The double meaning of the word "vision" is relevant here. What Beckett fails to clarify is the relationship between the vision he intends to express in the play and that of his central, visionless character.

The suggestion of a belief in a punitive exterior force is brought into much clearer relief in the mime *Act Without Words I*, which follows *Endgame* as a kind of corollary. The man is flung backwards on stage from the wings. He hears a whistle from offstage, first from the right, then from the left, but each time he goes off in answer to it, he is flung back on. A palm tree descends from the flies to tantalize him by offering shade from the dazzling sunlight and then closing up like a parasol. A carafe of water appears but eludes all his efforts to reach it. He wants to hang himself but the bough of the tree folds down against the trunk. He wants to cut his throat with a pair of scissors, but they are whisked away before he can do it.

Kott says the mime is like the Book of Job without

an optimistic ending. It is also without any assumption of justice in heaven. The powers in control are sadistic and irresponsible. The only way to avoid frustration is by inaction. The mime ends with the man ignoring the whistles from above, ignoring the proffered shade and ignoring the dangling carafe. He lies on the stage, looking at his hands.

This is a much simpler allegory of the human condition than we get in any of the plays or novels, but the immobility for which the nameless protagonist settles is related to the immobility from which so many of his heroes start, while the ones who can move often come to find movement more and more difficult as the action progresses. Molloy starts off hobbling friskily about on crutches; by the end of his narrative he can hardly move at all. Moran is not lame when he starts off in pursuit of Molloy, but the longer he goes on looking for him, the more he comes to resemble him. Malone is unable to get out of bed, the Unnamable is static, Bom in *How It Is* can only crawl about on the mud and he becomes more and more a voice, less and less a body.

Beckett himself has often drawn attention to this tendency of his to represent humanity in terms of broken-down old creatures lacking at least one limb or one faculty.

Mahood is no worse than his predecessors. But before executing his portrait, full length on his surviving leg, let me note that my next vice-exister will be a billy in the bowl, that's final, with his bowl on his head and his arse in the dust, plump down on thousand-breasted Tellus, it'll be softer for him. Faith that's an idea, yet another, mutilate, mutilate, and perhaps some day, fifteen gen-

> erations hence, you'll succeed in beginning to look
> like yourself, among the passers-by. In the mean-
> time it's Mahood, this caricature is he.

In the novels, part of the result is to focus the investi-
gations of the hero's inquiring mind away from the
frustrations of external circumstances on to the mind
itself. The more the body is pared down and immobilized, the less there is left to get in the way of our
seeing just a mind working. The preoccupation is still
with the conditions of our existence and our relations
to the absolute—but without looking at them in terms
of relationships with other people and external events.
We are in the cave, but Beckett brings into play all
the searchlights at his disposal.

In his basic attitude to the relationship between the
body and the mind, Beckett is very Cartesian. For
Descartes (who is the hero of Beckett's poem *Whoroscope*) the mind is purely spiritual and the body
purely material and mechanical, but he was never
able to solve the problem of how one affects the other.
His disciples, Malebranche and Geulincx, explained it
as an illusion which God induces—mind cannot act on
matter, but He makes it seem to. I am not moving my
hand because of a message traveling from my brain
through my nerves but because God is simultaneously
moving my hand and making me think that I am
doing it. This means that God has preordained everything that happens and all human ideas of cause and
effect are so much fiction. And since the self cannot
have any influence on external functions, its only
scope and significance would lie within itself.* Profes-

---

* The "baroque Rationalism" of Malebranche and Geulincx is
described very well in Richard N. Coe's book on Beckett.

sor Hugh Kenner in *Samuel Beckett: A Critical Study* quotes a maxim of Descartes which might almost have been the maxim of an early Beckett hero:

> To endeavor always to conquer myself rather than fortune, and change my desires rather than the order of the world . . . and this single principle seemed to me sufficient to prevent me from desiring for the future anything which I could not obtain, and thus render me contented.

Without endorsing the Cartesian philosophy, Beckett is obviously very attracted not only by the ideas but also by the prose—especially Geulincx's—and by the tone of the argument, which he affectionately parodies in his early novels and in the theological arguments in *Waiting for Godot*. But what is more important is that some of the actions and the inaction of Beckett's characters become a lot clearer when considered in the light of Cartesian reasoning. The time lapse between the decision and the action is a reminder that the connection between the two isn't necessarily a simple one. With Pozzo thrashing about on the ground, unable to get up, Vladimir and Estragon still take time for a careful discussion about whether or not they should help him. And at the end of the play they say "Let's go" and stay exactly where they are. The intention to move doesn't necessarily correspond with the initiation of appropriate actions in the appropriate limbs. Characters in the novels often find it necessary to analyze with extraordinary attention to detail the movements of a hand or a foot, as if it were an independent entity.

Exactly the same thing happens in *Endgame*.

Hamm tells Clov to go, and instead of moving he heaves a great groaning sigh. When Hamm remonstrates, "I thought I told you to be off," the answer is "I am trying." And it is the same with the parents. When Nell wants to go back into the garbage can, she doesn't go back and she doesn't know why she doesn't. At the end of the play, after Clov has finally decided to leave Hamm, he packs and stands there ready to go, but never actually gets himself to the point of going.

These repetitive and protracted delays are very basic to Beckett. It's hard enough to proceed in a straight line when you know where you're going, but impossible when you aren't going anywhere. It's not only the characters who don't know how they are going to get through the next five minutes, Beckett doesn't either, and he is quite happy to take the audience into his confidence about this. In *How It Is*, he keeps measuring how much more he has to write before he gets to the end. As in the novels of Laurence Sterne, any diversion is to be welcomed, any digression pursued. But Beckett is unlike Sterne in his reluctance to enter into the picture in his own person, and in the novels there is a vast amount of confusion between himself and the personas he uses to speak through. He makes an attempt to resolve this in *The Unnamable*, but of course he is still using a persona to make the attempt.

> It's of me now I must speak, even if I have to do it with their language, it will be a start, a step towards silence and the end of madness, the madness of having to speak and not being able to, except of things that don't concern me, that don't

count, that I don't believe, that they have
crammed me full of to prevent me from saying
who I am, where I am, and from doing what I
have to do in the only way that can put an end to
it, from doing what I have to do. How they must
hate me! Ah a nice state they have me in, but still
I'm not their creature, not quite, not yet. To tes-
tify to them, until I die, as if there was any dying
with that tomfoolery, that's what they've sworn
they'll bring me to. Not to be able to open my
mouth without proclaiming them, and our fellow-
ship, that's what they imagine they'll have me re-
duced to. It's a poor trick that consists in ramming
a set of words down your gullet on the principle
that you can't bring them up without being
branded as belonging to their breed. But I'll fix
their gibberish for them. I never understood a
word of it in any case, not a word of the stories it
spews, like gobbets in a vomit. My inability to
absorb, my genius for forgetting, are more than
they reckoned with. Dear incomprehension, it's
thanks to you I'll be myself, in the end. Nothing
will remain of all the lies they have glutted me
with. And I'll be myself at last, as a starveling
belches his odourless wind, before the bliss of
coma. But who, they? Is it really worth while inquiring? With my cogged means? No, but that's
no reason not to. On their own ground, with their
own arms, I'll scatter them, and their miscreated
puppets. Perhaps I'll find traces of myself by the
same occasion. That's decided then. What is
strange is that they haven't been pestering me for
some time past, yes, they've inflicted the notion of
time on me too. What conclusion, using their
methods, am I to draw from this? Mahood is silent, that is to say his voice continues, but is no
longer renewed. Do they consider me so plastered

> with their rubbish that I can never extricate my-
> self, never make a gesture but their cast must
> come to life? But within, motionless, I can live,
> and utter me, for no ears but my own. They
> loaded me down with their trappings and stoned
> me through the carnival. I'll sham dead now,
> whom they couldn't bring to life, and my mon-
> ster's carapace will rot off me.

This is all very reminiscent of schizophrenic perse-
cution mania—the belief in a hostile "they" who want
to deprive the victim of his identity by forcing their
words and concepts on to him. The quest for the self
is what is important, but it is impossible to pursue the
quest without using words, and since the words are
their words, this is testifying to them. What comes
closest of all to the ravings of the inmates of Dr. Rokeach's Ypsilanti is the confident determination to out-
wit them in the end, to remain intact, to spite them by
surviving and to survive by shamming dead.

Of course the madness is partly in focus, but only
partly, and we, the readers or the audience, are partly
beckoned inside, partly expected to watch it from outside. This is one of the many big differences between
Endgame and *King Lear*,* where the madness per-
vades the play but never takes over. You always know
exactly where Shakespeare stands in relation to it. The
other big difference, of course, is in the actual texture
of the language.

> That's right. (*Exit Clov. Pause.*) Me to play. (*He
> takes out his handkerchief, unfolds it, holds it*

---

* Kott is doing Beckett no service in considering the two
plays as if they were on the same level of greatness. Beckett has
often suffered unintended harm at the hands of critics who talk
about him in the same breath as Shakespeare or Dante.

spread out before him.) We're getting on. (*Pause.*) You weep, and weep, for nothing, so as not to laugh, and little by little . . . you begin to grieve. (*He folds the handkerchief, puts it back in his pocket, raises his head.*) All those I might have helped. (*Pause.*) Helped! (*Pause.*) Saved. (*Pause.*) Saved! (*Pause.*) The place was crawling with them! (*Pause. Violently.*) Use your head, can't you, use your head, you're on earth, there's no cure for that! (*Pause.*) Get out of here and love one another! Lick your neighbour as yourself! (*Pause. Calmer.*) When it wasn't bread they wanted it was crumpets. (*Pause. Violently.*) Out of my sight and back to your petting parties! (*Pause.*) All that, all that! (*Pause.*) Not even a real dog! (*Calmer.*) The end is in the beginning and yet you go on. (*Pause.*) Perhaps I could go on with my story, end it and begin another. (*Pause.*) Perhaps I could throw myself out on the floor. (*He pushes himself painfully off his seat, falls back again.*) Dig my nails into the cracks and drag myself forward with my fingers. (*Pause.*) It will be the end and there I'll be, wondering what can have brought it on and wondering what can have . . . (*he hesitates*) . . . why it was so long coming. (*Pause.*) There I'll be, in the old refuge, alone against the silence and . . . (*he hesitates*) . . . the stillness. If I can hold my peace, and sit quiet, it will be all over with sound, and motion, all over and done with. (*Pause.*) I'll have called my father and I'll have called my . . . (*he hesitates*) . . . my son. And even twice, or three times, in case they shouldn't have heard me, the first time, or the second. (*Pause.*) I'll say to myself, He'll come back. (*Pause.*) And then? (*Pause.*) And then? (*Pause.*) He couldn't, he has gone too far. (*Pause.*) And then? (*Pause. Very agitated.*)

All kinds of fantasies! That I'm being watched! A rat! Steps! Breath held and then . . . (*he breathes out*). Then babble, babble, words, like the solitary child who turns himself into children, two, three, so as to be together, and whisper together, in the dark. (*Pause.*) Moment upon moment, pattering down, like the millet grains of . . . (*he hesitates*) . . . that old Greek, and all life long you wait for that to mount up to a life. (*Pause. He opens his mouth to continue, renounces.*) Ah let's get it over! (*He whistles. Enter Clov with alarm-clock. He halts beside the chair.*) What? Neither gone nor dead?

Beckett himself seems to have King Lear's mad scenes somewhere at the back of his mind, but this is very thin broth by comparison. There's no universality here and precious little poetry. Instead of a rousing condemnation of humanity by a hero who has been driven before our eyes to the limits of human endurance, we have the desiccated, cynical, lonely musings of a bitter old man who has rejected humanity for reasons which have never been brought into the picture. "Lick your neighbour as yourself!" and "Back to your petting parties!" express a disgust with other people that has never been justified in the play. We are simply made to assume that they are all dead. But, as always in Beckett, it's not so much people as the conditions of living that come in for the heavy fire.

The rather abstruse reference to the "old Greek" is to Zeno, who used the example of a heap of millet to show the discontinuity between movements in space and time on the one hand and reality on the other, the essence of reality being infinity. If you pour half a sack of millet into a heap, and then add half of what is left in the sack to the heap, and then go on taking half of what is left in the sack to add to the heap, you will never have all the millet in the heap because you are moving in space and time. In infinity, the sack could be emptied, the heap could be completed. The implication for Hamm is that however long you go on living, the minutes never add up to a life because the end is always ahead of you. But for him, the problem is already abstracted away from external reality. All he wants to do is be "alone against the silence and . . . the stillness. If I can hold my peace, and sit quiet." The repetitions of words and phrases that mean almost exactly the same thing is symptomatic of meaning that is being tricked out to take up as much space as possible. The point has been made some time ago, and this speech has very little to add to it. The self-pity would work if we could look at him from outside, either as a clown or as a character, or if we could identify more with him. But by opting away from life, he has cut himself off both from reality and from the audience. Instead of being made into a good joke, as it was in *Waiting for Godot*, the boredom of waiting for the end, waiting for nothing to happen, is becoming a bore.

Whatever the defects of *Endgame*, it has elements in it, moments of blackness, that work very powerfully on an audience. The main source of their power is Beckett's integrity, his unremitting determination not to distort anything that he can say in the process of saying it. Neither in the theatrical images that he creates nor in the speeches that make extended statements are there any concessions to the expectations of the audience or to the conventions of the medium. The writing is naked, embarrassing, sincere, and theatrically incomplete. But this very incompleteness increases the spectator's need to project his own despair into the spaces in the play, embracing it as a statement he would never have been able to make for himself of a vision which seems to overlap with his own. So the solipsism is shared and the failure to focus it is bypassed.

All That Fall

Beckett's radio plays are far more visual than his stage plays. As a medium, theater has never stimulated him into exploring very many of its potentialities. What is usually said is that Beckett isn't interested in "that kind of theater," that his plays belong to "Anti-theater" or the "Theater of the Absurd." It is very easy to beg the question and hide all his limitations by sticking a label right over them. I think we stand a much better chance of arriving at a fair balance sheet of strengths and weaknesses if we side-step this pressure that always arises to herd writers into groups and schools.

An austere economy has always been his principle. Scenically, a single tree is the greatest extravagance he has ever allowed himself. Never a change of scene. Never a cast of more than four. Not much color. No pageantry. No sweep or scale in terms of physical movement. Progressively (or regressively) less and less movement of any kind. If the theater embarrasses Beckett by offering so much, radio delights him by putting nothing at his disposal except space for voices and sounds. In *All That Fall*, his first radio play, he builds up a most vivid picture of old Maddy Rooney's

63

journey along the country road towards the railway station. We hear music playing in a house, animal noises from sheep, birds, cows and cocks, a hinny neighing, a bicycle with its bell and squeaky brakes, a truck with its thunderous rattle, a car with all the repertoire of noises cars make, approaching and receding, door-slams, the engine ticking over, the starter and the throttle, the gears grinding, and we even get the squawk of a hen being killed. If Beckett's object had been to include more sound effects than any previous radio play, he could hardly have done better.

Of course, he doesn't limit himself to using sounds naturalistically:

> The wind—(*brief wind*)—scarcely stirs the leaves and the birds—(*brief chirp*)—are tired singing. The cows—(*brief moo*)—and sheep—(*brief baa*)—ruminate in silence. The dogs—(*brief bark*)—are hushed and the hens—(*brief cackle*)—sprawl torpid in the dust.

Here he is playing around, but there are several passages where the words and sounds are dovetailed together imaginatively to create a very good impression of movement—particularly at moments when movement is difficult, as it is when Tommy the porter helps to heave the massive Maddy Rooney out of Mr. Slocum's car. Or when she gets Miss Fitt to help her up the steps.

> (*Sound of her toiling up steps on Miss Fitt's arm.*) This is worse than the Matterhorn, were you ever up the Matterhorn, Miss Fitt, great honeymoon resort. (*Sound of toiling.*) Why don't they have a hand-rail? (*Panting.*) Wait till I get some air. (*Pause.*) Don't let me go! (*Miss Fitt*

hums her hymn. After a moment Mrs. Rooney
joins in with the words.) . . . the encircling
gloooom . . . (*Miss Fitt stops humming*) . . . tum
tum me on. (*Forte.*) The night is dark and I am
far from ho-ome, tum tum—

There is altogether much more movement in the play
than we are used to in Beckett, and it is built into the
picture, subtly, in considerable detail, and, above all,
unobtrusively. The eternal problem of the radio dramatist is to avoid speeches like, "Look, Mrs. Jones is
coming round the corner." Beckett makes it easier for
himself by having a blind man (once again*) as a
protagonist, which means not only that he has to be
told what's happening and where he is but also that
he's liable to translate any movement he senses near
him into words.

Have you been drinking again? (*Pause.*) You are
quivering like a blancmange. (*Pause.*) Are you in
a condition to lead me? (*Pause.*) We shall fall
into the ditch.

As in the novels, Beckett himself takes great pleasure in the movement he relays to us so vividly, but,
as in the novels, his characters don't. Maddy's dragging footsteps are the most recurrent sound effect of
all and, moving with so much difficulty, she resents
having to move at all.

How can I go on, I cannot. Oh let me just flop
down flat on the road like a big fat jelly out of a
bowl and never move again! A great big slop

---

* Another reason for the frequent recurrence of blindness in
Beckett's work is that it forces the victim to look inwards, and
seeing nothing he may see Nothing.

thick with grit and dust and flies, they would have to scoop me up with a shovel.

Tired of moving, tired of her body, tired of her life, her one wish is for dissolution.

What's wrong with me, what's wrong with me, never tranquil, seething out of my dirty old pelt, out of my skull, oh to be in atoms, in atoms! (*Frenziedly.*) ATOMS!

Like Murphy, she'd love to fade away into nothingness.

Would I were lying stretched out in my comfortable bed, Mr. Barrell, just wasting slowly, painlessly away, keeping up my strength with arrowroot and calves-foot jelly, till in the end you wouldn't see me under the blankets any more than a board. (*Pause.*) Oh no coughing or spitting or bleeding or vomiting, just drifting gently down into the higher life, and remembering, remembering . . . (*the voice breaks*) . . . all the silly unhappiness . . . as though . . . it had never happened.

Sometimes the dialogue makes her seem like an object, as Watt seemed when Mr. Hackett and Tetty first saw him.

Tetty was not sure whether it was a man or a woman. Mr. Hackett was not sure that it was not a parcel, a carpet for example, or a roll of tarpaulin, wrapped up in dark paper and tied about the middle with a cord.

Maddy uses exactly the same image.

Thank you, Miss Fitt, thank you, that will do, just prop me up against the wall like a roll of tarpaulin and that will be all, for the moment.

And she also becomes very much like an object when she is pushed out of the car.

Dan, too, her blind husband, has much the same antipathy towards movement.

> MR. ROONEY: Do you know what it is, I think I shall retire.
> MRS. ROONEY (*appalled*): Retire! And live at home? On your grant!
> MR. ROONEY: Never tread these cursed steps again. Trudge this hellish road for the last time. Sit at home on the remnants of my bottom counting the hours—till the next meal. (*Pause.*) The very thought puts life in me! Forward, before it dies!

But then Dan has an antipathy towards everything. He hates children and often has the urge to kill the little boy who acts as his guide. There is one long speech in which he lists all the expenses he runs into by going to work and establishes to his own satisfaction that he would add considerably to his income by staying in bed all day. But he completes his joyless accountancy with another long speech that lists all the ordeals of staying in the house.

> Dusting, sweeping, airing, scrubbing, waxing, waning, washing, mangling, drying, mowing, clipping, raking, rolling, scuffling, shovelling, grinding, tearing, pounding, banging and slamming. And the brats, the happy little healthy little howling neighbours' brats.

All That Fall is also very different from Beckett's stage plays in the way it registers the passage of time. There are plenty of passing phrases like "the remnants of my bottom" and "the once female shape," or stoic references to the constant fact of aging.

> MR. SLOCUM: Are you going in my direction?
> MRS. ROONEY: I am, Mr. Slocum, we all are.

The dialogue is rich in references to dung and other surviving debris from past physical processes or seasonal changes. At one point Dan thinks he can smell a dead dog in the ditch, but Maddy tells him it's rotting leaves.

> MR. ROONEY: In June? Rotting leaves in June?
> MRS. ROONEY: Yes, dear, from last year, and from the year before last, and from the year before that again.

The stress on physical deterioration is unremitting. Everyone that Maddy meets is asked more or less the same question—"How's your wife?" or "What news of your poor son?" or "How's your poor father?" So the picture builds up that everyone is suffering from something, which is sometimes more painful, sometimes less, but for the most part, it neither gets better nor worse. As for Dan, the worse he gets, the better he seems to feel. The loss of his sight was a great fillip to him and he thinks that if only he could go deaf and dumb, too, he might live to be a hundred.

But whereas in *Waiting for Godot* and *Endgame*, the slow passage of time was brought out by the fact that none of the characters had anything to do, they are all going somewhere in *All That Fall*. Even in the scene at the railway station, waiting for the train to come in, we get very little stress on the fact of waiting. Throughout the whole play, there is tension and suspense of the kind Beckett usually avoids. During Maddy's journey to the station, there is the uncertainty of whether she will get there in time. While she is there, we have the mystery of why the train is fifteen minutes late on a thirty minute run, and when it comes in, the mystery of the delay still isn't cleared up. Not until the end of the long section dealing with Dan and Maddy's journey home, the end of the play, in fact, do we learn a small child has fallen out of a carriage and been killed under the wheels. The question that never gets answered conclusively is whether Dan killed him. We are given plenty of circumstantial evidence to suggest that he did and that all his long description of the journey is a lie, but this isn't the point of the play.

What is the point of the play? Maddy and Dan are both alike in their hatred of movement and in their hatred of most of the things that make up the substance of living. But Maddy also hates the fact that she is childless. Once she had a child, Minnie, who died.*

. . . (*brokenly*): In her forties now she'd be, I don't know, fifty, girding up her lovely little loins, getting ready for the change . . .

This is negative enough in its tone and certainly it is not without irony that she is made to look at the

---

* Unless Minnie is a fantasy.

"pretty little woolly lamb" crying to suck its mother. But the basic regret is meant to be taken seriously. In a speech that lifts her rather out of character, she tells Dan how she once went to a lecture by a "mind-doctor" in the hope that he would shed some light on her "lifelong preoccupation with horses' buttocks." During the lecture, she says, the doctor told the story of how he once had to give up the case of a little girl he was treating because he couldn't find anything wrong with her, except that she was dying. (At this juncture, the point seems to be the familiar one that we are all dying because we are all alive and there is no cure for that.) But then shortly after he stopped treating her, the child died. The trouble with her, he says, was that she had never really been born. And this reduces Maddy to tears, thinking of the child that she hasn't given birth to.

Today we are more accustomed than audiences were in 1957 to narratives that leave the ends loose. Beckett has helped to change literary habits, and of all his plays *All That Fall* has perhaps the greatest apparent perversity in frustrating expectations it has itself created. Instead of solving the mysteries, the last scene merely shifts the conversation over to God and gives us a series of hints which promise enlightenment but withhold it. Dan asks Maddy who the preacher is tomorrow, and the name she mentions, Hardy, is a name we have heard before from Mr. Tyler, the man with the bicycle, who used to go climbing with Hardy and once saved his life. Tomorrow, Hardy's text is going to be "The Lord upholdeth all that fall and raiseth up all those that be bowed down." The quotation sends Dan and Maddy into a fit of wild laughter and they seem closer to each other in mood than ever before, but at this moment Jerry catches up with them, bringing an object which Dan has dropped.

> MRS. ROONEY: It looks like a kind of ball. And yet it is not a ball.
> MR. ROONEY: Give it to me.
> MRS. ROONEY (*giving it*): What *is* it, Dan?
> MR. ROONEY: It is a thing I carry about with me.

He refuses to say any more than that about it, and he tries to stop Maddy from asking Jerry what delayed the train.

> MR. ROONEY: Leave the boy alone, he knows nothing! Come on!
> MRS. ROONEY: What was it, Jerry?
> JERRY: It was a little child, Ma'am.
> (*Mr Rooney groans.*)
> MRS. ROONEY: What do you mean, it was a little child?
> JERRY: It was a little child fell out of the carriage, Ma'am. (*Pause.*) On to the line, Ma'am. (*Pause.*) Under the wheels, Ma'am.
> (*Silence. Jerry runs off. His steps die away. Tempest of wind and rain. It abates. They move on. Dragging steps, etc. They halt. Tempest of wind and rain.*)

And that is all.

Krapp's Last Tape

In his book on Proust, Beckett had put forward the thesis that the perceiving mind is itself changing so fast that the realization of yesterday's aspirations can provide no gratification to the self of today. In *Krapp's Last Tape* he has produced the perfect slide rule for measuring a character's past against his present self. He started writing the play after hearing the Irish actor Patrick Magee on the radio. His dry, gravelly, sepulchral voice excited Beckett so much that he wrote the play for him, inventing an old man who for over forty years has been keeping a sort of diary on tape and is now in the habit of playing his past tapes to help him get through the day. When he talks back at his old tapes, it produces what amounts to a dialogue between two Krapps at a considerable remove from each other in time. This is better than any kind of flashback device as a means of confronting one self with the other—and the audience with both. The effect is like reflections inside a prism made of one man's experience. Thirty years ago Krapp was already in the habit of playing tapes from his past, and he was already laughing at the self he had been

twelve years before that. And now he starts a new
tape with the comment:

> Just been listening to that stupid bastard I took
> myself for thirty years ago, hard to believe I was
> ever as bad as that.

So we are still inside the prism. There is exactly the
same kind of retrospect in the present and there is the
prospect of a future in which Krapp will listen to the
tape he made today, mocking at the self that he hears
on it from the vantage point he will then have at-
tained, which will seem to be so different. The whole
process is circular, but the circles could go on in a
straight line for ever, like bicycle wheels.

It's all like a literal translation into dramatic terms
of T. S. Eliot's *Burnt Norton*.

> Time present and time past
> Are both perhaps present in time future,
> And time future contained in time past.
> If all time is eternally present
> All time is unredeemable.
> What might have been is an abstraction
> Remaining a perpetual possibility
> Only in a world of speculation.
> What might have been and what has been
> Point to one end, which is always present.
> Footfalls echo in the memory
> Down the passage which we did not take
> Towards the door we never opened
> Into the rose-garden. My words echo
> Thus, in your mind.

Of course, Eliot's conception of eternity is a religious
one, but his belief in moments of illumination is not

unlike Beckett's belief in moments where involuntary memory is in operation. For both of them, these moments give us the only genuine insight into reality. Everyday reality, as we experience it, is a fiction. But for Beckett, and for his characters, there is no possibility of grace, no escape from the deadening awareness of the meaningless passage of time.

For Krapp, who is a writer, the only reality is words. His own past self is only real for him in the form of words on a tape, and the pleasure he enjoys most in the present is the pleasure of words. Within the first minute of the action, we see him relishing the word "spool." "Spooool," he croons. And the moment gets mentioned later on in his tape for today.

> Revelled in the word spool. (*With relish.*) Spooool! Happiest moment of the past half-million.

Otherwise he has very little to record. He looks at the notes he has made on the back of an envelope and crumples it up.

> Nothing to say, not a squeak. What's a year now? The sour cud and the iron stool.

He still has footfalls echoing in his memory down passages which he did not take.

> Effie . . . (*Pause.*) Could have been happy with her, up there on the Baltic, and the pines, and the dunes. (*Pause.*) Could I? (*Pause.*) And she?

And he still has sex with a "bony old ghost of a whore."

Couldn't do much, but I suppose better than a kick in the crutch. The last time wasn't so bad.

He also recently made a last effort at churchgoing, but went to sleep and fell off the pew. Sometimes, in the night, it occurs to him that it might be worth making a last effort at "living" as other people do it, having relationships, but when he starts to talk about this into the recorder, he gets very impatient with himself. "Once wasn't enough for you." And he suddenly wrenches the tape off the machine, throws it away and again plays the thirty-year-old tape that he has already played twice, with the passage about love-making.

I lay down across her with my face in her breasts and my hand on her. We lay there without moving. But under us all moved, and moved us, gently, up and down, and from side to side.

The first time we heard this passage, we didn't know what came just before it on the tape.

I said again I thought it was hopeless and no good going on and she agreed, without opening her eyes.

So it isn't until the second time the tape is played that we learn that even this cherished experience was set from the beginning in a context of failure. And it isn't until the third time of playing, at the very end of the play, that we hear the lines that come just after it on the tape.

Past midnight. Never knew such silence. The earth might be uninhabited.
(*Pause.*)
Here I end this reel. Box—(*pause*)—three, spool —(*pause*)—five. (*Pause.*) Perhaps my best years are gone. When there was a chance of happiness. But I wouldn't want them back. Not with the fire in me now. No, I wouldn't want them back.

And this is how the play ends, with Krapp motionless, staring in front of him and the tape running on in silence.

The image of the old man and his tape-recorded memories has the same sort of profoundly disturbing resonance as the central image in *Waiting for Godot*. It's a very short play, only twelve pages of script, but it succeeds completely in making the ripples spread out a long way around it in the audience's mind.

Where it doesn't succeed completely is where Beckett never succeeds completely—in bringing the central figure into focus. The only play or novel that escapes this criticism is *Waiting for Godot* where there is no single central character. By knocking up against each other so much, Vladimir and Estragon each harden the outline around the other. But with Krapp, the problem is how far do we take him as a particularized character, a lonely old eccentric, and how far as Everyman? There is the usual, unmistakable aspiration towards making statements about the nature of the self, about time and memory and the human condition, even though Beckett isn't pushing them this time, as he did in *Endgame*. But in so far as the tape on Krapp's machine is an image of the mind, coiling backwards and forwards in time, endlessly repeating itself with the same memories, hopes, anxieties, preoccupations, this must be valid in relation to everyone's mind, not just Krapp's. In Beckett's view, Krapp is by no means untypical in failing over relationships, in finding a complete discontinuity between past, present, and future selves, or in getting trapped hopelessly in a continuous present that spreads out endlessly and repetitiously into the past and the future. What causes the blurring of focus is that the respects in which Krapp is typical don't quite settle down into the same picture as the respects in which he is highly abnormal.

To begin with, like all Beckett's heroes from Belacqua onwards, he is given a formidable intellect, rather like Beckett's own in its scornful fastidiousness. And like all Beckett's heroes, Krapp prefers solitude to sex or sociality. At one time he lived with a woman, but he was glad when that was over. At the age of thirty-nine he celebrated his birthday alone in a wineshop, sitting in front of the fire with his eyes closed. He had already been suffering for some time from a bowel condition, which made drinking bad for him, but of the preceding eight thousand hours, he calculated that he had spent seventeen hundred on licensed premises in the "flagging pursuit of happiness. Unattainable laxation." The tape recording sneers at what it calls his youth and thanks God that it's over.

But what makes this withdrawal necessary? Such memories as he has of himself as a child are unhappy ones. Comparing himself with old Miss McGlome "who usually sings at this hour," he asks himself,

> Shall I sing when I am her age, if I ever am? No. (*Pause.*) Did I sing as a boy? No. (*Pause.*) Did I ever sing? No.

This inevitably raises the question of why he was unhappy and why he withdrew from other people. But
there's no answer to be found in the play. You have to
turn to *Malone Dies*.

> Live and invent. I have tried. I must have tried.
> Invent. It is not the word. Neither is live. No
> matter. I have tried. While within me the wild
> beast of earnestness padded up and down, roar-
> ing, ravening, rending. I have done that. And all
> alone, well hidden, played the clown, all alone,
> hour after hour, motionless, often standing, spell-
> bound, groaning. That's right, groan. I couldn't
> play. I turned till I was dizzy, clapped my hands,
> ran, shouted, saw myself winning, saw myself los-
> ing, rejoicing, lamenting. Then suddenly I threw
> myself on the playthings, if there were any, or on
> a child, to change his joy to howling, or I fled, to
> hiding. The grown-ups pursued me, the just,
> caught me, beat me, hounded me back into the
> round, the game, the jollity. For I was already in
> the toils of earnestness. That has been my disease.
> I was born grave as others syphilitic.

In this aspect, Krapp is yet another incarnation of
Murphy, Molloy, Malone, Mahood, the familiar Beckett solitary. The same inclination to withdraw from
contact with other people was made into a kind of
manifesto in the book on Proust.

> The attempt to communicate where no communi-
> cation is possible is merely a simian vulgarity, or
> horribly comic, like the madness that holds a con-
> versation with the furniture. Friendship, accord-
> ing to Proust, is the negation of that irremediable
> solitude to which every human being is con-

demned. Friendship implies an almost piteous acceptance of face values. Friendship is a social expedient, like upholstery or the distribution of garbage buckets.

The rejection of friendship later becomes less militant and more painful, when he faces up to the question of whether it may be not a refusal but a disability, or at least whether the refusal and the disability may be twins. But, as Beckett makes the Unnamable say, "It's myself I hear, howling behind my dissertation."

When Martin Held was rehearsing the part of Krapp under Beckett's direction, he saw that, as with so many of the characters, there was a strong connection with Beckett himself. "I did one thing which made me very nervous of offending him. When I have my hand on the table,"—crooking the knuckle of one finger—"this is Beckett. He can't move his hand. I groped my way towards it very gradually, doing a bit more of it each day until he noticed it and said 'Good'."*

Beckett insisted there should be no resignation in the character, even when he imagines that death is waiting for him in the darkness at the edges of the room. "When Krapp looks backwards . . . when he's about to switch the machine on and he thinks he hears something behind him and he listens and slowly turns round, I knew just what Beckett meant when he said 'Old Nick's there. Death is standing behind him and unconsciously he's looking for it.' Or when he listens, switches off and sinks away into dreams. He told me the character was eaten up by dreams. But without

* Interview with Ronald Hayman in *The Times* (London) 25 April 1970.

sentimentality. There's no resignation in him. It's the end. He sees very clearly that he's through with his work, with love and with religion."

Some of the other aspects of Krapp's character are put quite effectively into a critical perspective. Hearing the word "viduity" on the tape, Krapp has to stop the machine and consult a dictionary to find out what it means—"state or condition of being or remaining a widow or widower." The word "laxation" on the tape does not produce any reaction in the listening Krapp, but the one halt is enough to characterize him as someone who uses obscure words when there is no need to. But in the play's opening stage direction we see that Krapp is described as a "wearish" old man. Which is typical of the difficulties in the way of audience identification. There is no way of knowing how far the hero's characteristics are part of the character that Beckett is giving him or how far they are characteristics of Beckett which he is sharing.

Embers

Embers is the play in which Beckett most clearly marks down the central character as mad, but the madness spreads from the character to infect the whole body of the play that contains him. First we hear Henry giving himself orders as if his body and his mind were independent organisms: "On." "Stop!" "Down!" and it is only the second time he gives himself each order that we hear the sound of his boots walking on a shingle, or the silence as they stop, or the slither of shingle as he sits on it. He goes on talking incessantly and soon we gather that it is something much more sinisterly compulsive than mere garrulousness. Ever since his father was drowned, he has been obsessed by the sea, always wanting to be near it but frightened to go into it and unable to bear the sound of it, which is in his head all the time, whether he is near it or not. So he keeps talking, to himself if necessary, telling himself stories, anything to make a noise, just to drown the sound of the sea in his head.

Since Endgame, with its blurring of subjective vision and external reality, and with the ambiguity of Clov's involvement in Hamm's madness, Beckett has been concerned more and more with monologue. Krapp's tapes, Henry's obsession and Winnie's sand pile in *Happy Days* are all devices that get the character into the position of talking of himself, to himself, and for himself.

With Henry, as with the others, we are not allowed to stand back and look at the madness—or listen to it—from a distance. We are forced inside it. "Who is beside me now?" he asks himself, and answers his own question.

> An old man, blind and foolish. (*Pause.*) My father, back from the dead, to be with me. (*Pause.*) As if he hadn't died.

We guess that there is no one there, but in a radio play, silence, absence and nonexistence all make themselves felt in the same way. It is only when a character talks that he is real for the audience. In *All That Fall*, Maddy was made humorously aware of this when she spoke up for herself after a silence.

> MRS. ROONEY: Do not imagine, because I am silent, that I am not present, and alive, to all that is going on.
> MR. TYLER (*to Miss Fitt*): When you say the last train—
> MRS. ROONEY: Do not flatter yourselves for one moment because I hold aloof, that my sufferings have ceased. No.

And with Henry's father, even when we go on hearing nothing from him, we can never be sure that he isn't going to speak. So in effect the medium works in collusion with the madness and forces us from moment to moment into conceding the possibility that Henry may be talking to a real person, and Beckett, who rejects any such easy differentiation between the real and the unreal, makes us abandon our own conception of reality, at any rate for so long as we are listening to *Embers*.

He does this by means of sound effects. Like a radio Prospero, Henry is endowed with the power of conjuring up any sound effect he fancies. "Hooves!" he orders, and we have an obliging clatter of horses walking on a hard road. When the sound fades away he orders it back and issues more instructions.

> Train it to mark time! Shoe it with steel and tie it up in the yard, have it stamp all day! (*Pause.*) A ten-ton mammoth back from the dead, shoe it with steel and have it tramp the world down!

But this time there are no answering sound effects. Does this mean that Henry is trying to hear the sounds inside his own head and failing? Possibly, but you cannot satisfactorily translate the play into meaning of this sort. There is no discernible consistency about it, even within its own terms. We are neither quite taken into the madness nor quite left outside it but kept swinging uncomfortably between the two positions.

One ambiguity that has confused two such sympathetic critics as Hugh Kenner and Martin Esslin is that when Ada's voice is heard talking to Henry, it is difficult to be sure whether Ada is "really" present or whether we are being made to hear a voice that Henry is imagining. There is not much evidence either way. Just before Ada speaks, Henry imagines himself in conversation with their daughter, Addie, and he imitates the child's voice.

> What turned her against me do you think, the child I suppose, horrid little creature, wish to God we'd never had her, I use to walk with her in the fields, Jesus that was awful, she wouldn't let go my hand and I mad to talk. "Run along now, Addie, and look at the lambs." (*Imitating Addie's voice.*) "No papa." "Go on now, go on." (*Plaintive.*) "No papa." (*Violent.*) "Go on with you when you're told and look at the lambs!" (*Addie's loud wail. Pause.*)

When Ada speaks, it is an actress's voice that we hear, but when Henry calls out Ada's name, just before her first line, it is done in just the same way as he conjures up sound effects.

> HENRY: Ada. (*Pause. Louder.*) Ada!
> ADA (*low remote voice throughout*): Yes.
> HENRY: Have you been there long?
> ADA: Some little time. (*Pause.*) Why do you stop, don't mind me. (*Pause.*) Do you want me to go away?

Another point is that none of her movements produce any sounds. We did not hear shoes on the shingle before she came and there is a stage direction specially to stipulate that there should be no sound as she sits. Perhaps the object of the ambiguity is to suggest that ultimately it is not very important whether Ada is there in the flesh or only as an image and a sound inside Henry's head. At one point towards the end, she asks him:

ADA: Who were you with just now? (*Pause.*) Be-
fore you spoke to me.
HENRY: I was trying to be with my father.
ADA: Oh. (*Pause.*) No difficulty about that.
HENRY: I mean I was trying to get him to be with
me . . . I was asking him if he had ever met you,
I couldn't remember.
ADA: Well?
HENRY: He doesn't answer any more.
ADA: I suppose you have worn him out. (*Pause.*)
You wore him out living and now you are
wearing him out dead. (*Pause.*) The time comes
when one cannot speak to you any more.
(*Pause.*) The time will come when no one will
speak to you at all, not even complete strangers.
(*Pause.*) You will be quite alone with your
voice, there will be no other voice in the world
but yours. (*Pause.*) Do you hear me?

Perhaps part of the point is that it does not much
matter whether she is saying this now, or said it once
in the past, or never said it at all. What matters is that
it is present in Henry's consciousness, just as the statements from the past are present for Krapp on his
tapes. And what matters still more is that it is true.
This is how the dialogue goes on.

HENRY: I can't remember if he met you.
ADA: You know he met me.
HENRY: No, Ada, I don't know, I'm sorry, I have
forgotten almost everything connected with you.

The time has already come when Henry is alone with
his own voice. Even if Ada is physically present, very
little gets through to him of what she says, except
what he knows already or what he wants to hear. And

in this he is very much like the perceiving mind, as described in *Proust*, which cannot admit the reality that it encounters, except by imposing its own preconceived notions on it.

> Normally we are in the position of the tourist whose aesthetic experience consists in a series of identifications and for whom Baedeker is the end rather than the means.

But there is one thing that does get through to Henry from what Ada says, and this is crucial. She did meet his father, on the day that the old man was drowned, and from her description of the events of that day it becomes obvious to Henry that the drowning was suicide. For a long time beforehand, his father had been sitting on a rock looking out to sea. The whole family had been upset that day because of Henry. His bed hadn't been slept in, no one knew where he was and his sister had been threatening to throw herself off the cliff. Ada, who had arranged to go bathing with Henry, left without seeing him. This is why he has forgotten whether Ada and his father ever met.

I doubt whether anyone could assimilate this fully just from hearing the play once on the radio. But if my reading is correct, the enlightenment that Ada brings to Henry couldn't possibly come from a voice already present inside his head. She is more like a messenger in a Greek tragedy, providing new information which enables the hero to unravel the truth about a past catastrophe, precipitating a new catastrophe by giving him a new awareness of his own guilt.

Before Ada came, Henry was fairly contentedly talking to himself, telling himself stories, talking to the image of his father in his mind. But when Ada is about to go, he pleads with her to stay with him a bit longer, even if she won't speak, even if she won't listen, just to be there with him. He cannot bear to be alone with his guilt. He already knew that his father wished he hadn't had him, just as he wishes he hadn't had his daughter. (Giving birth to another human being, committing someone to imprisonment in the continuum of living is, for Beckett, one of the unforgivable sins.) At the end of the play, Henry is left alone, looking out to sea just as his father was, the day he drowned, and perhaps Henry too is thinking of the same escape. In the meantime, hardly able to bear the burden of guilt without Ada's palliating presence, and confined, like Krapp, to the world of his own voice, Henry falls back on his madness and goes on telling himself the story he started before Ada came.

As in *All That Fall*, where the surname Hardy was a clue to a linkage of component ideas, here the surname Holloway is a common factor between the story Henry is telling himself and the story Beckett is telling us about Henry. Holloway is the name of his doctor. When he complains of the noises in his head, Ada keeps telling him to see Holloway. And in the story he tells himself, Holloway is also a doctor. The other character in the story is Bolton, an old man in a red dressing gown, waiting in front of a dying fire for Holloway to come. It is after midnight. Holloway is also an old man and finally he arrives with his little black bag after his journey through the snow, but Bolton won't tell him why he sent for him. All he says is, "Please! PLEASE!" The flames of the fire die out and the old doctor tries to keep warm in front of the embers, vainly asking Bolton what he wants. He offers him an injection, he threatens to go, but each time he is met with the same inarticulate incomprehensible appeal, "Please! PLEASE!" The pleading becomes weeping and the embers grow cold and the old doctor has to turn away, unable to meet the look in Bolton's "drowned" eyes. The wordplay is obviously important, just as the pun on "waste" is important in the play's closing lines as Henry is looking in his diary for the next few days.

> This evening . . . (*Pause.*) Nothing this evening. (*Pause.*) Tomorrow . . . tomorrow . . . plumber at nine, then nothing. (*Pause. Puzzled.*) Plumber at nine? (*Pause.*) Ah yes, the waste. (*Pause.*) Words. (*Pause.*) Saturday . . . nothing. Sunday . . . Sunday . . . nothing all day. (*Pause.*) Nothing, all day nothing. (*Pause.*) All day all night nothing. (*Pause.*) Not a sound. (*Sea.*)

Happy Days

In *Happy Days* we are faced with a bosomy fifty-year-old blonde buried up to her waist in the center of a low mound in an expanse of scorched grass. In Act One she can move her arms but in Act Two she is buried up to her neck, unable even to move her head. In effect, the play is almost a monologue, but there is also Winnie's husband, Willie. Most of the time he is out of sight on the far side of the mound and when he speaks at all, it is usually to utter one syllable. He can still move about, on all fours, but he doesn't crawl fully into sight until the end of the play. His chief function in the action is to provide a strictly theoretical possibility that he is listening to Winnie. She knows he is not and most of the time she is talking neither for him nor to him, but his presence makes her speeches something different from what they would be if she were entirely alone.

Where Beckett reverses his normal practice is in putting a character in the center of the picture who is female, extravert and unintelligent. Willie's temperament is very much more like that of the normal Beckett hero. From Winnie's point of view it is a matter of

> no zest—for anything—*no interest—in life*—poor dear Willie—sleep for ever—marvellous gift.

But Winnie's point of view is not at all the same as Beckett's point of view. For the first time we are not asked to identify with the attitude of the central character. The play creates a comic pathos around Winnie's misplaced optimism, her inexhaustible capacity for happiness in circumstances that would make any reasonable creature miserable.

In a curious way, *Happy Days* is an extension of *Endgame*, just as *Endgame* was of *Waiting for Godot* —a reincarnation of the less interesting of the two pairs of characters. This time, instead of developing the master-slave relationship, Beckett devotes the play to a couple who are not quite so old as Nagg and Nell, but no less commonplace. In *Endgame*, Nell was the character who interested Beckett least and had least to say. Winnie doesn't interest Beckett at all, but she has an enormous amount to say.

The triviality of her mind is underlined (as if it needed underlining) by the triviality of her actions. They are not only small in scale—as they are bound to be with her body half-buried in sand—they are petty, and the play constantly emphasizes how inappropriate they are to her situation. We see her cleaning her teeth, filing her nails, putting on lipstick and adjusting her hat, rather like the joke about the Englishman putting on a dinner jacket to eat all by himself in the desert. Her incessant, fussy actions are marked out by stage directions even more meticulous than the ones in *Waiting for Godot*.

Pause. Willie resumes fanning. Winnie lays down glass and brush, takes handkerchief from bodice, takes off and polishes spectacles, puts on spectacles, looks for glass, takes up and polishes glass, lays down glass, looks for brush, takes up brush and wipes handle, lays down brush, puts handkerchief back in bodice, looks for glass, takes up glass, looks for brush, takes up brush and examines handle through glass.

Most of her actions are actions which are part of anyone's daily routine, but because of her situation, they all appear utterly incongruous and pointless—clasping her hands in prayer, checking through possessions in her bag, inspecting her teeth and gums in a looking-glass, polishing her spectacles, shaking out a handkerchief prior to wiping away a reminiscent tear, drinking medicine.

Beckett makes very much the same sort of point about characters to whom these elements of the daily routine are important in his mime *Act Without Words II*, which, like the first *Act Without Words*, is a tense and very gloomy summing up of the whole of life. On a long, narrow, brightly lit platform at the back of a darkened stage, we see two sacks and a pile of clothes. Prodded by a stick from the wings, a man gets out of the first sack and, pausing to brood between each action, prays, swallows a pill from a bottle, dresses, chews a carrot, spits it out, moves the sack, prays, undresses and crawls back into the sack. The man who, when prodded, gets out of the other sack, moves much more precisely and keeps consulting a large watch between each action. He does exercises, cleans his teeth with a brush from his pocket, rubs his scalp, combs his hair, dresses, brushes his clothes and his hair, looks at himself in the mirror, chews his carrot with relish, consults a map and a compass, moves both sacks in the same direction as the first man, and after undressing, doing his exercises again and repeating the business of rubbing his scalp, combing his hair and brushing his teeth, he crawls back into the sack. Then the other man is prodded into action again.

The man who broods is like Willie, but the brisk man, like Winnie, is shown to be the victim of habit, as Beckett defines it in the book on Proust—a kind of shell people grow to defend themselves against full awareness of the "suffering of being."

> Habit is a compromise effected between the individual and his environment, or between the individual and his own organic eccentricities, the guarantee of a dull inviolability, the lightning-conductor of his existence. Habit is the ballast that chains the dog to his vomit. Breathing is habit.

The argument goes on to define a polarity between suffering and boredom:

> The fundamental duty of Habit, about which it describes the futile and stupefying arabesques of its supererogations, consists in a perpetual adjustment and readjustment of our organic sensibility to the conditions of its worlds. Suffering represents the omission of that duty, whether through negligence or inefficiency, and boredom its adequate performance. The pendulum oscillates between these two terms: Suffering—that opens a window on the real and is the main condition of

the artistic experience, and Boredom—with its host of tophatted and hygienic ministers, Boredom that must be considered as the most tolerable because the most durable of human evils.

The heroes of the novels all suffer—Winnie is incapable of suffering in this sense, and she is incapable of remembering. Not one of her "happy memories" is a real memory in Beckett's or in Proust's sense.

> My first ball! (*Long pause.*) My second ball! (*Long pause. Closed eyes.*) My first kiss! (*Pause. Willie turns page. Winnie opens eyes.*) A Mr. Johnson, or Johnston, or perhaps I should say John*stone*. Very bushy moustache, very tawny. (*Reverently.*) Almost ginger! (*Pause.*) Within a toolshed, though whose I cannot conceive. We had no toolshed and he most certainly had no toolshed. (*Closes eyes.*) I see the piles of pots. (*Pause.*) The tangles of bast. (*Pause.*) The shadows deepening among the rafters.

She is entirely a victim of Time.

> The individual is the seat of a constant process of decantation, decantation from the vessel containing the fluid of future time, sluggish, pale and monochrome, to the vessel containing the fluid of past time, agitated and multicoloured by the phenomena of its hours. Generally speaking, the former is innocuous, amorphous, without character, without any Borgian virtue. Lazily considered in anticipation and in the haze of our smug will to live, of our pernicious and incurable optimism, it seems exempt from the bitterness of fatality: in store for us, not in store in us.

But for all her pernicious, incurable optimism, Winnie is no longer able to expect any freedom in the future. What imprisons her is her own past. The narrator in *The Unnamable* took very much the same view of Time, as being something that refuses to pass, something that gradually buries you.

> The question may be asked, off the record, why time doesn't pass, doesn't pass, from you, why it piles up all about you, instant on instant, on all sides, deeper and deeper, thicker and thicker, your time, others' time, the time of the ancient dead and the dead yet unborn, why it buries you grain by grain neither dead nor alive, with no memory of anything, no hope of anything, no knowledge of anything, no history and no prospects, buried under the seconds, saying any old thing, your mouth full of sand.

But stated like this, the image has much more resonance than it has in *Happy Days*, stated in bad visual terms.

In fact the whole play makes a great many points that Beckett has made before, and it does not make them anything like so well. There are bells to signal the beginning and the end of the day, for the glare of the sunlight is unremitting here, and although Winnie is looking forward to the next holiday from consciousness with less impatience than Vladimir and Estragon were waiting for night to fall, or Hamm for the game to be over, the feeling is much the same. Her fantasy wish of leaving the earth altogether, of being sucked up into the blue is reminiscent of Maddy Rooney's desire for dissolution and of *Murphy*, where the old man's kite took on a symbolic association to the life leaving Murphy's body. The way Winnie starts her day by giving herself orders:

> Begin, Winnie. (*Pause.*) Begin your day, Winnie

is exactly like Henry in *Embers*. Her teeth and gums, like the invalids in *All That Fall*, are "no better, no worse," and it reminds us of *Endgame* when we learn that she is running out of supplies. We see her drinking the last of the medicine and there is very little toothpaste or lipstick left.

> Running out—(*looks for cap*)—ah well—(*finds cap*)—can't be helped—(*screws on cap*)—just one of those old things—(*lays down tube*)—another of those old things—(*turns towards bag*)—just can't be cured—(*rummages in bag*)—cannot be cured.

But all this is too forced and explicit. Even her consciousness of her own physical deterioration and even her resignation, both of which are absolutely central to the character, are overstated.

> (*examines handle of brush, reads*)—genuine . . . pure . . . what?—(*lays down brush*)—blind next —(*takes off spectacles*)—ah well—(*lays down spectacles*)—seen enough—(*feels in bodice for handkerchief*)—by now.

Of course it is part of the point that Winnie is talking for talking's sake. She's afraid of silence, afraid of the vacuum.

What day? (*Pause.*) Words fail, there are times
when they even fail. (*Turning a little towards
Willie.*) Is that not so, Willie? (*Pause. Turning a
little farther.*) Is not that so, Willie, that even
words fail, at times? (*Pause. Back front.*) What is
one to do then, until they come again? Brush and
comb the hair, if it has not been done, or if there
is some doubt, trim the nails if they are in need of
trimming, these things tide one over.

But the fear of silence has nothing of the pregnancy
that it has in the radio plays, where existence consists
entirely in spoken words, or in the novels, where the
stream of words corresponds entirely with the inner
action, and silence, however much it's longed for,
would mean extinction. On the stage a character can
exist in silence, but not in a radio play or a first-person
narrative.

But Winnie is not just less of an intellectual than
any other leading character of Beckett's, she is also
much less articulate, and the writing is forced down to
a very low level when the point comes for her to fall
back on telling herself a story. This is what she has to
do when all else fails, as it does in Act Two, when she
thinks Willie has either left her or got stuck in his
hole. The story is about a little girl, Milly, undressing
her doll. The technique of elaborating the story is very
much the same as in the novels. The only thing that
matters is to keep going, so the choice of details is
arbitrary but, as in free association, one thing leads to
the next and *something* is evolved, the implication
being that anything is as good as anything else to fill
the vacuum, or to fend off awareness of "the suffering
of being." The character in the story is always very
much like the narrator. The child in Winnie's story is
patently herself and she tells the story to herself as to

a child. But it is not a very good story and she cannot keep it up for very long.

When she gives up, she is prey to the noises she hears in her head, just like Henry, Murphy, and Malone, but unfortunately her noises are not as credible as their noises, and neither is her desperation. The basic trouble is that Beckett has given Winnie a consciousness which simply isn't adequate for what he's trying to do through it. The weakest passage of all comes when he puts semiphilosophical speculations into her mouth about the sounds she hears.

> Sounds. (*Pause.*) Like little . . . sunderings, little falls . . . apart. (*Pause. Low.*) It's things, Willie. (*Pause. Normal voice.*) In the bag, outside the bag. (*Pause.*) Ah yes, things have their life, that is what I always say, *things* have a life. (*Pause.*) Take my looking-glass, it doesn't need me.

This is an echo of a feeling Malone had when he was a child that trees and grass and sand all made noises of their own, and it is also Winnie's version of the Sartrean *en-soi*, but the persona simply doesn't fit with the preoccupations or the compulsions.

> I used to think there was no difference between one fraction of a second and the next. (*Pause.*) I used to say . . . (*pause*) . . . I say I used to say, Winnie, you are changeless, there is never any difference between one fraction of a second and the next. (*Pause.*) Why bring that up again? (*Pause.*) There is so little one can bring up, one brings up all. (*Pause.*) All one can . . . (*pause*) . . . I can do no more. (*Pause.*) Say no more. (*Pause.*) But I must say more. (*Pause.*) Problem here.

The whole equation of words with consciousness and consciousness with existence is much less relevant to a woman like Winnie than to an intellectual, and particularly to an intellectual engaged in the business of writing, as so many of Beckett's central characters are. Though Krapp is the only professional writer, the activity of writing bulks large for Molloy, who is writing the book in his mother's room, where a man comes each week to take away the pages and to give him money; for Moran, who is writing his report for Youdi; and for Malone, who is penciling his deathbed thoughts into an exercise book. Hamm and Henry have both been occupied for some time with the stories that they are making up, and for both of them the story is a means of dragging their own past into the present, partly as a method of filling the emptiness and partly in a neurotic attempt to get control over it. But the points that Beckett makes are much more valid in relation to artists, intellectuals and schizophrenics than to average people engaged in ordinary jobs and activities, and in ordinary sexual and social relationships.

It was certainly a mistake for him to make a woman like Winnie into a heroine. As a character in a play she would only be tolerable if she were involved in action and relationships. By burying her in sand and showing that her habitual optimism survives, Beckett makes a valid dramatic point, but it is one that could have been made in a brief sketch, without inflicting Winnie on us for quite so long. He may have succeeded in creating a character with less resemblance to himself than any of his previous heroes, but the price he paid for this success was too high.

Words and Music and Cascando

Beckett's next two radio plays *Words and Music* and *Cascando* were very much slighter than his first two. They play around humorously with the possibilities of the medium but not in order to make any kind of statement, even of the sort that *All That Fall* and *Embers* make. In fact, these later pieces are not so much plays as sketches. In both of them Beckett hits on very imaginative devices, breaking up an interior monologue into separate voices and making Music into a "character" with a will of its own. This is skittish and amusing. What is disappointing, after becoming so familiar with his equation of words with consciousness and consciousness with existence, is that nothing more comes of it when he personifies "Words." In the novels, in *Happy Days* and in *Embers*, we have had innumerable references to voices inside a character's head. Sometimes the voices are attributed to "them." Usually it is left in doubt whether the words come from inside the self or outside, or whether "they" are "dictating" words which they are making the narrator think of as his own. But instead of using his new radio techniques, as he could have, to explore this uncharted question of provenance, he contents himself with a few virtuoso arabesques.

In *Words and Music*, Words, otherwise known as Joe, and Music, otherwise known as Bob, are both at the disposal of a character called Croak, who has not yet arrived when the action begins. We hear a small orchestra tuning up and we hear Words giving himself a trial run on the theme of sloth. The sentences that come out are repetitive and almost meaningless, like padding in a schoolboy essay.

> Sloth is of all the passions the most powerful passion and indeed no passion is more powerful than the passion of sloth, this is the mode in which the mind is most affected and indeed—

Croak's arrival is heralded by the sound of shuffling carpet slippers. Apologizing for being late with an incomprehensible mutter about "the face on the stairs," he announces the theme for tonight, which is love. Words responds with exactly the same speech that we heard him rehearsing, substituting the word "love" for the word "sloth." Croak's displeasure is signaled by the thump of a club on the ground. Music is now given a chance. Music can understand everything that is said to it in words but expresses itself only in sounds, so now we hear soft music with "great expression." Words groans so loudly in protest that Croak has to make Music play louder, which ruins all expression. Words is given a second chance but overplays his part, and Music, on a second attempt, does no better. Disappointed, Croak proposes an alternative theme, Age, and after abortive attempts from both Words and Music, Croak gets them to collaborate,

Words singing, Music accompanying. After a number of false starts and a great deal of prompting by Music, they come out with a simple little song about age and a face seen in the ashes of a fire, the face of a woman.

> Who loved could not be won
> Or won not loved
> Or some other trouble.

Uncomfortable in singing, Words goes back to speech. He talks on about the face, refusing all Music's offers of melody and accompaniment. It would have been so much better, he says, to see the face "in the light of day," but it is something that the face is so recurrent as an image in the consciousness.

> Flare of the black disordered hair as though spread wide on water, the brows knitted in a groove suggesting pain but simply concentration more likely all things considered on some consummate inner process, the eyes of course closed in keeping with this, the lashes . . . (*pause*) . . . the nose . . . (*pause*) . . . nothing, a little pinched perhaps, the lips . . .

Wretchedly, Croak now identifies the girl as Lily. Words talks on about

> the great white rise and fall of the breasts, spreading as they mount and then subsiding to their natural . . . aperture.

And Music illustrates this. Croak becomes more and more anguished and listens reluctantly as Words goes on into a rhetorical description of life and color flooding back into the features of the face. He is now much more willing to collaborate with Music, and, with accompaniment, sings twice a rather obscure little lyric which seems to be about the working of unconscious memory that can provoke this backward movement "through the trash," taking you without words, without sense, without need, to "one glimpse of that wellhead." But Croak cannot stand it and shuffles off, sad and speechless, leaving Words and Music alone together as they were at the beginning. But now Words, becoming more than mere words, starts to share Croak's emotion, imploring Music to repeat the theme of the song. The play ends with a deep sigh.

Of course radio is more suited to monodrama than the stage is. If your concern is with expression in terms of different voices inside one head, this cannot be achieved so well when the actors are visible. Even if you reduce your performers to static heads imprisoned in urns, they are palpably separate. On the air, they are not.

Just as Croak and Words represented two different parts of the same remembering mind, so, in *Cascando*, the storyteller is broken down into two component voices. The script calls one The Opener and the other Voice, and again, music is used more or less as a character. So The Opener has two "doors" at his disposal. He can open either the door for Voice or the door for Music or both together.

> They don't see me, they don't see what I do, they don't see what I have, and they say, He opens nothing, he has nothing to open, it's in his head.
> I don't protest any more, I don't say any more,

> There is nothing in my head.
> I don't answer any more,
> I open and close.

What we hear when he opens the door for Voice is a repetitive and half-incoherent sequence of incomplete phrases, rather like dots in a pointillist painting. Part of the time, Voice speaks about its own desire to finish, to have done, to tell just one more story and then stop, sleep. Often in the past there has been the same feeling—just get this one finished and then stop. But each time he has finished one, he has immediately started on the next, because the last one was never the right one, and the present one always is. Which is what he believes now.

As he goes on, the picture is formed impressionistically of an old man, Woburn, waiting for night to fall. And when it does, he goes out, down towards the sea. He walks with a stick, sometimes falling, perhaps on purpose, his face in the mud, but each time gets up and struggles on.

> What's in his head . . . a hole . . . a shelter . . . a
> hollow . . . in the dunes . . . a cave . . . vague
> memory . . . in his head . . . of a cave . . .

We are not told where he is going or what his intention is, but it is obvious he doesn't want to be seen, because there are broken phrases about the lights being too bright. He gets into a boat and puts out to sea

> heading nowhere . . . for the island . . . then no
> more . . . elsewhere . . . heading anywhere . . .
> lights—

The boat has no tiller, no thwarts, no oars and he is sucked out to sea, with his face in the bilge, clutching the gunnels. He might have got at least some help in finding his bearings from the lights in the sky above, if only he would look up, but he keeps his head down. He passes the island and drifts out into the open sea. The lights of the land vanish behind him and the voice leaves him drifting, clinging on, and reassuring itself that this time it really was the right story. There will be no more. Only sleep.

Play

Beckett's next play for the stage, a one-act piece called simply *Play*, has all three characters throughout in the same position that Winnie ended up in, imprisoned up to their necks, not in sand this time but in urns, their necks held fast in the urns' mouths. But they don't speak to each other even to the extent that Winnie was speaking to Willie. The man and the two women are all talking about a triangular relationship in which they were involved together, but each one has a separate series of memories about it and although their speeches are counterpointed, the minds behind them are not even aware of each other, except in the past tense. The speeches are not made in reply to any previous speech, they are made into the void, and this too is in accordance with the growing tendency for Beckett's monologues to be less and less addressed to anyone in particular. In this respect the development in the plays is following the pattern set by the novels, which are also monologues. Moran was writing a report for Youdi; Malone was writing for himself, with the words following fast on the heels of

105

the thoughts; the Unnamable was not writing at all but talking to himself in the void.

> Where now? Who now? When now? Unquestion-ing. I, say I. Unbelieving. Questions, hypotheses, call them that. Keep going, going on, call that going, call that on.

Krapp's tapes were made only for himself, and Win-nie needed no cues to talk, except from the bells. In *Play*, Beckett uses a spotlight to cue the speeches by shining on the character who is to talk. He has to go on talking till the light moves off him on to the next. Most of the time, the light settles on a single face, but even when it is spread over all three they are still quite oblivious of each other.

Beckett's opening stage direction suggests that the actors should not respond immediately to the light.

> *At every solicitation a pause of about one second before utterance is achieved, except where a longer delay is indicated.**

The intention is that the light should act as a kind of inquisitor—this is why Beckett asks for a single spot, preferably located in the center of the footlights, which is to swivel rapidly from one face to the next.

The effect this creates is of three people trapped and passive in a limbo created by their own con-sciousness. Light is associated with consciousness and disquiet, while the darkness they long for would mean peace and silence. It is like the bells in *Happy Days* speeded up to a purgatorial pace, without any sugges-

---

* In his 1964 production at the National Theatre, George Devine ignored this.

tion at all of a natural rhythm of division into days. We are much further outside time than we were in *Waiting for Godot*. The cycle is unending. The audience is made to hear the whole play twice, and the dialogue is about to start all over again as the play ends. This is torture for the characters, who all long to make an end, to be finally free from the consciousness that provokes this nonstop flow of words and stories that search into the self and into the past, into the past which constitutes the self and into the self which consists of nothing but the past. It is like listening to Krapp's tape recorder without any freedom to wind forward or backward or switch off. These characters are in a hell which is quite unlike Sartre's in *Huis-Clos*. There the torture is in each individual's awareness that other individuals are aware of him. Here, all relationship between them is lodged securely in the past and each of the three prisoners is in the solitary confinement of his own continuous present.

Play represents the culmination of a steadily developing tendency in Beckett's stage plays to call on the actor to do less and less except talk—in fact to make the stage play more and more like a radio play. All we can see of these three actors is their heads. "They face undeviatingly front throughout the play. Faces so lost to age and aspect as to seem almost part of urns." Beckett also demands "faces impassive throughout. Voices toneless except where an expression is indicated." And the only expressions that are indicated are "faint, wild laugh" once for the second woman (W2), "vehement" once for W1, "hopefully" once for W2 and two peals of wild, low laughter for ıer. The man is required to hiccup several times but

to talk tonelessly throughout. In fact the star per-
former is the lighting operator.

Even though the whole of the dialogue is played
twice, it's impossible for an audience to form more
than a very rough idea of what it was that happened
between the three characters. The information is fed
to us in very short fragments, sometimes out of chron-
ological order, and it is hard enough to piece them
together even from reading the printed script. M
seems either to have been married to W1, or at any
rate living with her for some time before he started
the affair with W2. W1 gets suspicious and has him
shadowed by a detective, but W2 bribes the man so
that W1 is given no proof of the infidelity and all this
time M continues "as assiduous as ever" as a lover,
reassuring her that he loves her with all his heart and
could not live without her. With all her suspicions so
well assuaged, she is taken completely aback when
one morning he confesses to her about the affair. She
storms over to W2's house and threatens to kill her,
but W2 pretends not to know what she is talking
about and when W2 tells M about the incident, he
reassures her by saying that W1 is always making
threats to him about suicide. He manages to make it
up with W1, though without giving up W2, who now
becomes very jealous of his relationship with her rival.
He appeases her with exactly the same statement that
he made to W1, that he cannot live without her. He
believes himself to be telling the truth in both cases.

Both conciliated in the same way, both women make
the same proposal to him, that he should go away
with them. He puts them both off, pleading professional commitments, and carries on in exactly the
same way with both. Then something happens—we

are not told what—which makes him decide that it is all too much for him. He disappears out of the lives of both women and of course each one thinks that he has left her for the other, while the man later on comes to wonder whether the two of them have made friends with each other. The quality of the monologues changes at this point. All isolated now, the characters all become more conscious of their own consciousness, and each flash of the light brings on a new attack of guilt and anxiety. W1, who used to be the most self-righteous of the three, is the one who finds the isolation and the self-awareness hardest to bear. "Get off me," she keeps saying to the light. She comes to think that it only settles on her when she is lying. If only she could find the strength to tell the truth, she would be left in peace and darkness.

> Is it that I do not tell the truth, is that it, that some day somehow I may tell the truth at last and then no more light at last, for the truth?

Meanwhile W2 wishes for madness as a release from her self-consciousness, while both M and W1 become increasingly aware of their own consciousness, as if it were something seen from the outside—by the light.

> W1: Yes, and the whole thing there, all there, staring you in the face. You'll see it. Get off me. Or weary.
> (*Spot from W1 to M.*)
> M: And now, that you are . . . mere eye. Just looking. At my face. On and off.
> (*Spot from M to W1.*)
> W1: Weary of playing with me. Get off me. Yes.
> (*Spot from W1 to M.*)

M: Looking for something. In my face. Some truth.
In my eyes. Not even.
(*Spot from M to W2. Laugh as before from
W2 cut short as spot from her to M.*)
M: Mere eye. No mind. Opening and shutting on
me. Am I as much—
(*Spot off M. Blackout. Three seconds. Spot on
M.*)
M: Am I as much as . . . being seen?

All this is in the play, but no audience could possibly get all this out of it. With the light flashing from one face to the next and with the quick toneless delivery of the actors, it is theatrically a very confusing experience. All one's energy goes on trying to piece the story together, but Beckett's only interest in the story is as a stalking-horse for his study of what happens to the three consciousnesses once the man opts out of both relationships, condemning all three of them to solitude. Differently treated, this could have been very good material. Treated as it is, very little is communicated. Beckett himself has called the words "dramatic ammunition" and what happens is that the words and the fragments of story are used in a kind of assault on the audience. This is one outcome of the paradox of writing for the theater without believing in the possibility of communication.

Eh, Joe and *Film*

The more plays Beckett writes, the more he tends to exclude external action and to concentrate on reproducing the voices in his hero's head. His development as a dramatist can be seen as a battle between monologue and dialogue, with monologue winning more decisively at each engagement. *Eh, Joe* is his first piece for television, written in 1965 and broadcast by the BBC in March 1966. Instead of letting the medium push him into paying attention to external events, he carries on his habitual progress, inwards and downwards.

Joe is a Beckett hero of the familiar sort, a shabby, gray-headed solitary in his late fifties, wearing an old dressing gown and carpet slippers. At the beginning, we see him shutting himself up in his room, shutting the window, closing the curtains, shutting and locking the door, and drawing the hanging across inside it. Apart from these actions, he is passive throughout, sitting on the edge of his bed and never even speaking. There is a monologue going on inside his head, in a woman's voice, and it is this that we hear. All we see is his reactions to it and he does not react much. The script demands that the face should be practically motionless throughout, impassive except in so far as it reflects the mounting tension of listening to the voice. And there must be very little camera movement. The exact points at which the camera is to move are laid down by the script—always during a pause in the monologue. Apart from the movements around the room in the silence at the beginning, there are just nine movements for the camera, and in each one the camera gets about two inches closer to Joe's face, ending in a close-up. Beckett is very specific about the timing of the camera's movements.

> *Camera does not move between paragraphs till clear that pause (say three seconds) longer than phrases. Then two inches in say four seconds when movement stopped by voice resuming.*

Once again the script takes us inside the mind of a character who is probably insane. We only hear the one voice during the play but it refers to other voices that go on inside Joe's consciousness.

> You know that penny-farthing hell you call your mind . . . That's where you think this is coming from, don't you . . . That's where you heard your father . . . Isn't that what you told me? . . . Started in on you one June night and went on for years . . . On and off . . . Behind the eyes . . . That's how you were able to throttle him in the end.

Joe fights against the voices "throttling the dead in his head," but he is also afraid of what it might be like if there were no voices going on.

> Watch yourself you don't run short, Joe . . . Ever
> thought of that? . . . Eh, Joe? . . . What it'd be if
> you ran out of us . . . Not another soul to still . . .
> Sit there in his stinking old wrapper loving him-
> self.

He is afraid of that and he is afraid of the point he
sometimes reaches where the voices that he fights
against become unintelligible.

> Squeezed down to this . . . How much longer
> would you say? . . . Till the whisper . . . You know
> . . . When you can't hear the words . . . Just the
> odd one here and there . . . That's the worst . . . It
> should be the best . . . Nearly home again . . .
> Another stilled . . . And it's the worst . . . Isn't that
> what you said? . . . The whisper . . . The odd word
> . . . Straining to hear . . . Brain tired squeezing . . .
> It stops in the end . . . you stop it in the end . . .
> Imagine if you couldn't . . . Ever thought of that?
> . . . If it went on . . . The whisper in your head . . .
> Me whispering at you in your head . . . Things
> you can't catch . . . On and off . . . till you join us
> . . . Eh, Joe?

The other big fear is that he will hear God's voice in
his head. "Wait till he starts talking to you . . . When
you're done with yourself . . . All your dead dead."
Like the man in *Film*, who is also obsessive about shutting himself up in a room so that nothing and no one
could see him, Joe seems to want, above all, to escape
the confrontation that is inevitable—between his consciousness and himself. Again, as in *Play*, there is an
association between consciousness and light.

> Thought of everything? . . . Forgotten nothing?
> . . . You're all right now, eh? . . . No one can see

> you now . . . No one can get at you now . . . Why
> don't you put out that light? . . . There might be a
> louse watching you.

Because the action, such as it is, is all internal action,
the past merges inextricably into the present. The
voice itself is the voice of a woman who was in love
with Joe until she found someone better. He has been
loved a great deal by women, from his mother onwards.

> Such love he got . . . God knows why . . . Pitying
> love . . . None to touch it . . . And look at him
> now . . .

And there was one girl who killed herself for him.
This is the part of the story which is told in the greatest detail by the narrating voice—how she "lies down
with her face in the wash," fails to kill herself that
way, hasn't the courage to slit her wrist, takes sleeping
tablets and "lies down in the end with her face a few
feet from the tide" and "scoops a little cup for her face
in the stones." The image of a body face downwards
drifting into death is reminiscent of the story in *Cascando*, and so are the broken, impressionistic phrases
that go to make up the story.

Altogether, the script has a good deal in common
with the script Beckett wrote for his *Film*, which
stars Buster Keaton and was shown at the London
Film Festival in 1965. Not a word is spoken by the
hero—or by anyone else. It is about the Berkeleyan
equation of existence with the fact of being perceived
and, as in *Eh, Joe*, we just see one man shutting himself up in his room, intent on getting rid of any possi-

bility of being seen. He does not even want to have his image reflected by anything. He throws out the dog and the cat, puts a cloth over the birdcage and the goldfish bowl, covers up a looking-glass, tears up a picture of Christ, and turns the other pictures with their faces to the wall. But he still is not isolated from himself, and to show this another figure, also Buster Keaton, suddenly appears from nowhere and he starts up in terror at the confrontation. *Eh, Joe* begins with a series of shots in which we only see Joe from behind; the same trick is played all the way through *Film*, and we do not see Buster Keaton's face until the final moment, when we see it twice.

Come and Go, Breath, and Not I

More than any other living writer, Beckett deserves to have it said of him that each of his works could have been written only by him and only at the precise point in his development at which he actually wrote it. The least self-indulgent, the most austerely disciplined of artists, he also has tremendous energy and persistence. In his drama as in his fiction he has more than once reached a point which made critics think what he has sometimes thought himself—that he could not possibly penetrate any further along his reductionist line of development, because if he eliminated any more he would be left with nothing.

Beckett has not written either a full-length novel or a full-length play since 1961, when *How It Is* was published in France and *Happy Days* was produced in the United States. But he has gone on writing, cutting his own work ruthlessly, jettisoning all conventions about the length proper to a novel or a play. The fiction and plays he has produced have sometimes seemed fragmentary and have sometimes been written in fragmented sentences. He has perhaps a greater capacity than any of his contemporaries for concen-

116

trating on the voice inside his own head, not writing merely at its dictation, but not compromising in a way that falsifies the message. The voice does not worry about syntax and the writer has to edit as he transcribes; however, sometimes Beckett concentrates on preserving the rhythms and cadences, and sometimes on communicating the images, fleshing them out for the reader. But he never allows the rhythm to distract him from the image, and in the best works of this period, like the stage work *Not I*, each reinforces the other. Sometimes, though, the pursuit of an image can distract him from the timbre of the voice, as it does in *The Lost Ones*, the longest of these short prose works, which is almost like a latter-day *Purgatorio*. Human striving to understand human existence is represented by the image of a self-contained cylinder in which ant-like "searchers" are trapped, weakened by failing sight and energy, but compulsively devoting their existence in the pulsating half-light to climbing ladders or standing in lines, waiting their turn to search.

The five prose pieces which have appeared since *How It Is* are—I will give the English titles and the dates of the original (French) publication—*Imagination Dead Imagine* (1965), *Enough* (1966), *Ping* (1966), *Lessness* (1969), and *The Lost Ones* (1970). Beckett has described them as "residua," and in reply to a questionnaire sent to him by Brian Finney, who was preparing his *Since How It Is* (Covent Garden Press, 1972), a study of the later fiction, he has explained this word. "They are residual (1) Severally, even when that does not appear of which each is all that remains and (2) In relation to whole body of previous work." This would seem to be equally applicable to the three short plays *Come and Go* (1965), *Breath* (1969), and *Not I* (1972). Each seems to consist only of the residue of a longer work, much of which has been scrapped. *Come and Go* is a brief and rather sketchy piece about the reunion of three elderly spinsters who used to be friends at school and who are now reaching the end of their unsatisfying and pointless-seeming lives. There are only one and a half pages of dialogue followed by a whole page of notes on the staging.

Breath was possibly intended less as a play than as a joke. It was written on a postcard to Kenneth Tynan for his *Oh! Calcutta!* For five seconds we see miscellaneous rubbish, faintly lit. (Tynan unwarrantably included naked people among the rubbish.) A brief cry is followed by an intake of breath, which continues for ten seconds as the light brightens. Without becoming very bright, the light stays at the same level for five silent seconds and then, together with an exhalation, it takes ten seconds to fade. There is another cry, identical with the first, and after five seconds of silence the sketch is over. For some critics this was a masterly summary of the whole life span between birth and death, although Beckett's stage direction stipulates that each cry should be an "instant of recorded vagitus."

Not I is an incomparably more substantial achievement which triumphantly vindicates Beckett's application of his reductionist methods to the theater. By digging in his heels further than ever before in his refusal to exploit the rich visual potentialities of the theater, and by approximating more closely than ever before the condition of radio drama, he boomerangs back into creating one of the most strikingly theatrical images of modern drama. Most of the stage is in complete darkness. In mid-air we see a human mouth and about two inches of surrounding flesh, positioned about two feet higher than it would be if the woman were standing on the stage. Very dimly, at the side, we see a listening figure, covered from head to foot in a loose djellabah, its head slightly higher than the mouth. Apart from making four slight movements it will be motionless. The audience's attention will be riveted by the movements of the lips, teeth, and tongue as the words pour urgently, desperately, pathetically out of the mouth. The sound will seem to come in flashes, creating pictures inside our imagination as vivid, as compelling, and almost as full of movement as the pictures created by the words in *All That Fall*.

As in the dialogue that Voice has in the radio play *Cascando*, we get a half-incoherent series of incomplete phrases, but a story is spilled out spanning the whole of a creature's life, whether we regard it as a life that has already been fully lived or an idea of life entertained by something that has never managed even to begin living. The infant described at the outset is speechless, a "tiny little thing" that came "out . . . into this world" before its time. Its parents had no love and no time either for each other or for it. The experience that Mouth has to retail is so painful that even now, after about seventy years have passed, it is only possible for her to talk about herself in the third person. All four movements of the listening figure are movements of "helpless compassion," and are made at moments when Mouth seems to be about to say "I" but baulks at it—". . . what? . . . who? . . . no! . . . she!" is her refrain. And the gesture of compassion becomes smaller each time it is repeated.

The effect of depersonalization is heightened by the ambiguity about whether Mouth is alive or unborn or dead. She seems to be situated in a Limbo not unlike that of *Play*, with its three ex-lovers tormented by enforced retrospection on their interdependent lives; she, however, has always been unloved and alone. The three ex-lovers were not the first Beckett characters to be depersonalized and immobilized by having everything but their heads rooted somewhere out of sight. We have also had blind characters in dark glasses. Now, for the first time, Beckett obscures not just the eyes but all the upper part of the head. After we have been informed, in one terse phrase, that her lovelessness extended from infancy to the whole of her subsequent existence, we are briskly moved seventy years forward to the time when she

> . . . found herself in the dark . . . and if not exactly . . . insentient . . . insentient . . . for she could still hear the buzzing . . . so-called . . . in the ears . . . and a ray of light came and went

Associated as it is with consciousness, this light is reminiscent of the spotlight in *Play* and the pulsating light in *The Lost Ones*. Beckett also goes beyond what he did with all the maimed and paralyzed creatures in his earlier work: he makes her ignorant of whether she is standing or sitting or kneeling or lying. The brain and the insistent voice that seems to come from it are given an existence which scarcely depends on the body.

Once again the ontological question that Beckett's image suggests is put into a theological perspective. There are references to God and sin, while existence is

assumed to have an intention underlying it. One is "intended" to be having pleasure or "meant" to be suffering. Like Dan and Maddy Rooney, who were sent into
a fit of wild laughter by the quotation from which the
play takes its title—"The Lord upholdeth all that fall
and raiseth up all those that be bowed down"—Mouth
twice laughs at her own words when the notion of a
merciful God occurs. The only effort she is capable of
making towards understanding her own situation is in
terms of punishment. At the same time, the theological
speculation is effectively counterweighted by the drive
towards meticulous objectivity in observing subjective
phenomena. In *Imagination Dead Imagine* and *The
Lost Ones* the totally unrealistic central image is described with quasi-scientific precision. Mouth aspires
to equal accuracy when, for instance, she corrects
herself after speaking of buzzing in the ears:

> . . . not in the ears at all . . . in the skull . . . dull
> roar in the skull . . .

Come and Go and *Breath* were both attempts, in a
sense, to span the space between birth or childhood
and old age or death, but without anything like the
emotional weight of *Not I*. The ambiguity about where
Mouth is situated in time and space does not under-
mine Beckett's control over his material but helps it,
keeping the emotional facts judiciously out of focus.
When Mouth screams, for instance, it is in the middle
of a narrative passage about a period of being unable
either to move or to make any sound. The startling
screams the mouth then emits contradict the silence
that the narrative has just created, but we do not know
whether she discovered then that she could scream

after all, or whether the scream exists only in the Limbo present. In *Krapp's Last Tape* we find not just one detached point from which to look back on the evanescent pleasures and the protracted pains of past experience but a series of semi-detached points; here we find only the locus of a possible point.

The climax of the narrative comes when Mouth describes the dawning of the awareness that words were coming:

> ... a voice she did not recognise ... at first ... so long since it had sounded ... then finally had to admit ... could be none other ... than her own ... certain vowel sounds ... she had never heard ... elsewhere ... so that people would stare ...
> the rare occasions ... once or twice a year ... always winter some strange reason ...

The reference to winter also helps to suggest a span of time, for we have already had several references to April, springtime being associated with childhood. Flashing us backward and forward in time, deftly but indefinitely, the voice first tells us how she herself first came to hear it and then returns to the subject of silence, which reigned over her existence up to that moment. We get a vivid and grotesque impression of her shopping silently in a "supermart," handing in a list with her old black shopping bag, then waiting for it to be handed back to her, full. Then we come to the beginnings of her present alienation from herself: not catching everything that her voice was saying, she started trying to delude herself into thinking that it was not her own voice she was hearing. This is also what a writer does when he makes a voice from inside his own head into that of a character. This is where art and madness overlap.

The voice then brings us to an almost surrealist account of the renaissance of the mouth. As the narrative moves from the subject of the voice to the subject of the mouth we see in front of us, the impression is reinforced that the action is situated outside time, that the silence was death and the ensuing resurrection only a hideously partial one.

It would be very unwise to work out an exact meaning for the play in these terms, but there seems to be a connection with the premise of *Imagination Dead Imagine*.

> No trace anywhere of life, you say, pah, no difficulty there, imagination not dead yet, yes, dead, good, imagination dead imagine. Islands, waters, azure, verdure, one glimpse and vanished, endlessly, omit. Till all white in the whiteness in the rotunda. No way in, go in, measure.

Later on we shall find there are two bodies inside the Rotunda, but, on one level, it obviously represents the interior of the brain, and the narrative concerns the resurrection of the imagination after its own death. In *Not I*, we have, perhaps, an equivalent resurrection, but only for the mouth, the ultimate and inevitable theatrical image for the nonstop voice inside the head, the voice we are hearing, while what we see, pinpointed by a spotlight as if it were under a microscope, is a human mouth, not unlike our own; however, it is alienated, isolated; a moist pink tongue thrashes about like a dying fish inside a blubbery orifice that changes shape with every vowel sound, a helpless victim of the consciousness of pain that pours through it, an exact visual counterpart to the febrile rhythms of this agonized prose.

The woman is characterized as half-demented—habitually she stands about with her mouth half-open. The image in front of us also illustrates the story we are hearing when the voice refers to the birth cry that marked the beginning of her existence. The persistent rhythm of the short phrases that come out of the moving mouth also corresponds in a way to the buzzing she constantly hears inside her own head, just as the incessant sound of the sea is lodged irremovably inside the consciousness of Henry in *Embers*.

The one inexplicable riddle in the play is why the woman was taken to court. Thematically the reference to the courtroom is relevant to her feeling that she is probably being punished for something, but the introduction of an insoluble mystery into the narrative is rather reminiscent of the ending of *All That Fall*, and slightly irritating in much the same way. It introduces a kind of suspense that neither play needs. In *Not I*, the intensity generated by the sound of the voice and the spectacle of the moving mouth is so enormous that even this small vestige of plot is redundant.

STAGE PRODUCTIONS
IN NEW YORK

April 1956   *Waiting for Godot*, directed by Herbert
              Berghof, with Bert Lahr, E. G. Mar-
              shall, and Alvin Epstein, at John Golden
              Theatre.

January 1957 *Waiting for Godot*, directed by Herbert
              Berghof, with Geoffrey Holder and
              Earle Hyman, at Ethel Barrymore
              Theatre.

October 1957 *All That Fall*, a "concert" reading staged
              by Edward Greer, with Susan Steell,
              Liam Clancy, and Paul Ballantyne, at
              Carnegie Hall Playhouse. First U. S.
              performance.

January 1958 *Endgame*, directed by Alan Schneider,
              with Alvin Epstein, Lester Rawlins,
              P. J. Kelly, and Nydia Westman, at the
              Cherry Lane Theatre.

January 1960 *Krapp's Last Tape*, directed by Alan
              Schneider, with Donald Davis, at the
              Provincetown Playhouse.

September 1961   *Happy Days*, directed by Alan Schneider, with Ruth White and John C. Becher, at the Cherry Lane Theatre.

February 1962   *Endgame*, directed by Alan Schneider, with Ben Piazza, Vincent Gardenia, John C. Becher, and Sudie Bond, at the Cherry Lane Theatre.

March 1963   *Embers*, directed by Sidney Schubert Walter, with Paul Boesing and Dolores Tucker, at the Caffe Cino.

January 1964   *Play* (with Pinter's *The Lover*), directed by Alan Schneider, with Frances Sternhagen, Marian Reardon, and Michael Lipton, at the Cherry Lane Theatre.

June 1965   *Krapp's Last Tape*, directed by Alan Schneider, with George Bartenieff, at the Cherry Lane Theatre.

September 1965   *Happy Days*, directed by Roger Blin, with Madeleine Renaud (in French) and succeeded by Ruth White (in English), at the Cherry Lane Theatre.

April 1966   *Eh, Joe*, televised on National Educational Television, directed by Alan Schneider, with Rosemary Harris and George Rose.

October 1968   *Krapp's Last Tape*, with Donald Davis, and *Happy Days*, with Sada Thompson and Wyman Pendleton, both directed by Alan Schneider, at the Billy Rose Theatre.

June 1969 · *Breath*, performed as opening sketch in *Oh! Calcutta!*, directed by Jacques Levy, at the Eden Theater.

May 1970 · *Oh, Les beaux jours* (in French), directed by Roger Blin, with Madeleine Renaud and Olivier Hussenot, at the Barbizon Plaza Theatre.

May 1970 · *Endgame*, directed by Roberta Sklar, with Peter Maloney, Joseph Chaikin, James Barbosa, and Jayne Haynes (all of the Open Theater), at the Washington Square Methodist Church.

November 1970 · *MacGowran in the Works of Beckett*, adapted with the approval and advice of Beckett, presented by the New York Shakespeare Festival.

February 1971 · *Waiting for Godot*, directed by Alan Schneider, with Paul B. Price, Henderson Forsythe, and Anthony Holland, at the Sheridan Square Playhouse.

November 1972 · The Beckett Festival, offering *Act Without Words I*, with Hume Cronyn, and *Happy Days*, with Hume Cronyn and Jessica Tandy, and, on alternating nights, *Not I* (world premiere), with Jessica Tandy and Henderson Forsythe, and *Krapp's Last Tape*, with Hume Cronyn. All four plays, given at the Forum Theater, Lincoln Center, were directed by Alan Schneider.

BIBLIOGRAPHY

WORKS BY SAMUEL BECKETT

The Collected Works of Samuel Beckett. 16 vols. New York: Grove Press, 1970.

WORKS ABOUT SAMUEL BECKETT

Coe, Richard N. *Samuel Beckett.* New York: Grove Press, 1970.

Cohn, Ruby. *Samuel Beckett: The Comic Gamut.* New Brunswick, N.J.: Rutgers University Press, 1962.

Esslin, Martin, ed. *Samuel Beckett: A Collection of Critical Essays.* Englewood Cliffs, N.J.: Prentice-Hall, 1965.

Federman, Raymond. *Journey to Chaos: Samuel Beckett's Early Fiction.* Berkeley, Calif.: University of California Press, 1965.

Fletcher, John, and Spurling, John. *Beckett: A Study of His Plays.* New York: Hill and Wang, 1972.

Grossvogel, David I. *The Blasphemers: The Theatre of Brecht, Ionesco, Beckett, Genet.* Ithaca, N.Y.: Cornell University Press, 1970.

Hassan, I. H., *The Literature of Silence: Henry Miller and Samuel Beckett.* New York: Random House, 1967.

Hoffman, F. J. *Samuel Beckett: The Language of Self.* Carbondale, Ill.: Southern Illinois University Press, 1962.

Kenner, Hugh. *Samuel Beckett: A Critical Study*. Berkeley, Calif.: University of California Press, 1968.

Ludovic, J. *Pour Samuel Beckett*. Paris: Éditions de Minuit, 1966.

Marissel, André. *Beckett*. Paris: Éditions Universitaires, 1963.

Tindall, William Y. *Samuel Beckett*. New York: Columbia University Press, 1964.

INDEX